LOVE IS THE ROAD TO EVERYWHERE

YOU'VE JUST GOTTA SURVIVE IT

KIM PETERSEN

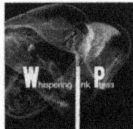

CONTENTS

LOVE is the ROAD to Everywhere

You've Just Gotta Survive it

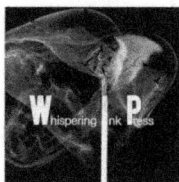

Whispering Ink Press

KIM PETERSEN

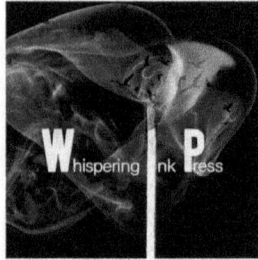

Cover Art & Formatting by Paradox Book Designs

For all of my lovers and for all of yours; past, present and future...

INTRODUCTION

Hey there!

If you have picked up this book because you're interested in reading about the messy ups and downs, and ins and outs of love and relationships, then you've hit the jackpot because that's exactly what you are going to get – love, sexuality, sacred connection and relationships.

Right here. Right now.

It is the real stuff that all of us have to deal with at some point in our lives. I mean, nobody gets away without experiencing the highs and lows of love in this lifetime.

Right? I feel you so much that I've been spending the better part of this year writing all about love in the most authentic way possible, and then publishing these little yarns for my readers on Medium.com – no holds barred. Just so that I can relate my personal experiences and therefore, better connect to you and bring us all closer together.

That's what love is all about – connectedness and togetherness; honesty, compassion and empathy.

I believe that by sharing our life experiences and insights about how we love, we are able to connect and understand each another in a much deeper and meaningful, organic way.

Are you ready to get deeply connected with me?

Let's survive this love-thing together.

Kim

WHAT MAKES A WOMAN UNFORGETTABLE?

It's not what you see in the media

There are so many mixed messages and pressure on what men expect from a woman nowadays. This is largely because we are bombarded with images that show us how to be desirable, and swamped with articles telling us what we should be wearing, doing, saying or not saying if we want men to find us alluring—unforgettable.

But we don't need to look like a supermodel to be unforgettable. We don't even need to be perfect. At all. A woman may do all the things that tells her how to attract a partner and still find herself alone.

The thing is, there is so much more that goes into a relationship than what a woman wears, the color of her hair or the shade of her lipstick. Sure, those things do contribute to first impressions, but what makes a woman unforgettable is much less about her clothes and more about who she is.

Quite a few years ago, a good friend jokingly referred to my ex-boyfriends as my "Old Flame Club" because they had a knack for unexpectedly showing up in my life years after the relationship had ended.

They would look me up on social media and ping me, or I'd hear from them through mutual friends who they had found and then requested my contact details. Thankfully, said mutual friends would always ask my permission before divulging my personal information.

Those who know me well have pretty good idea about how I feel about reconnecting with old boyfriends — Hell. No. Thanks.

Erm…

For the most part, I am uninterested in catching up with my exes. I'm not one of those people who are into attending school reunions either. That's just me. It's not that I have harsh feelings for past lovers or old friends, I do honor their place and the role they had in my life — it's more that I don't feel the need to rekindle past relationships.

You know when a relationship has run its course when you can look back with a sense of ease about how it ended. It just feels complete. Doesn't mean that that person no longer means anything to me— we shared time together and they will always be a part of me in some way.

Doesn't mean I want to reconnect, either.

The same goes for other kinds of relationships, too. When I divorced my first husband, I considered one of the perks of the split was that I would no longer have to deal with his mother.

Yeah. She was one of those cringe-worthy in-laws who frequently felt the need to impart her unwanted opinion and controlling advice on me at every opportunity.

Thirteen years on and she's still at it. Only, I let go of the hook — no longer do I feel obliged to answer her calls or possess the desire to stay connected.

Between you and me, she's one person I wish would forget me.

Hmm…I should be so lucky.

The friend who used to tease me about having an "old flame club" never understood why my ex-boyfriends were so interested in reviving a connection with me. Honestly, it was something that baffled me too.

"What is it about you that they can't forget?" she'd ask.

I'd reply with a shrug.

What did I know? I didn't consider myself overly special.

But I did know that it had nothing to do with my clothes or the way I styled my hair and more to do with what's going on on the inside. For those guys who I've loved and shared serious time with along the way, I have always given them the best part of me.

Just me.

All of us are unforgettable to someone and all of us will never forget someone.

Here's a few traits I believe makes a woman particularly unforgettable:

She has a passion for Life

Life is about living and experiencing new things.

A woman who is passionate about life and has a spark for exploration is one you won't forget in a hurry.

She laughs lots and doesn't take herself too seriously.

She's a free-spirit at heart who finds joy and fascination in the unlikeliest of things — it doesn't mean that she's always engaged in a wild venture or constantly pushing her comfort zone; but it does mean that she has an unforgettable zest for life that shines from the inside out.

She forms meaningful connections

She wants to know her man and she sees him, and she thrives on deep connection — not just in her romantic relationships, but also with the special people in her life, too.

Friends, family and co-workers — a combination of these connections.

Meaningful connections with other people outside of your relationship is healthy and helps to keep your romantic connection fresh and balanced.

For me, I was never the kind to build my entire existence around a man, encouraging him to spend time with his friends and cherishing my own space.

An unforgettable woman builds a life for herself and not for every romantic connection that shows up in her experience. Her meaningful connections are a part of who she is and a part of what makes her whole.

She's kind

She doesn't have to have a bleeding heart or try to save the world, but the kindness she shows to her loved ones and strangers alike says a lot about a woman — and it's contagious.

Her kindness sets off a chain reaction. Like a ripple effect, it makes you feel good. When we're around kind-hearted people, those qualities naturally emerge in us too and honestly, the world won't suffer from too much kindness.

An unforgettable woman is kind and caring — and although there may be times when her kindness is exploited or taken advantage of, her kindness is not easily forgotten.

She's got fire

She's gutsy yet vulnerable. Persistent but not a steamroller.

She knows what she wants and when life knocks her

down, she'll get back up, dust off her pants and forge ahead with renewed determination.

She realizes the value and growth that accompanies pain. She forgives easily and releases grudges because she knows that life is too short to hold onto negative emotions.

An unforgettable woman is a visionary; a dreamer who possesses the fire in her heart to fight and push for the life she wants.

An unforgettable woman is herself

Broad-mindedness is an alluring trait. So is authenticity.

She is uninterested in trying to be someone she is not and knows that the opinions others have of her is not her business.

An unforgettable woman is a person who is far from perfect but deep down she cannot be anything other than her real self.

She lives as herself.

Sometimes, she may be a bitch. She might even have a knack of getting under your skin and driving you crazy at times, but she'll love you even crazier and that's why you cannot forget her.

~

An unforgettable woman is the kind of woman who imprints on your soul and forever stays in your heart. If you shared real time and connection with her, then chances are she thinks you're pretty unforgettable, too.

2

WHAT MAKES A MAN AN UNFORGETTABLE LOVER?

It has nothing to do with the size of his wallet.

There are those among us who think of sex as nothing more than a means to an end. It often starts out this way, during those tempestuous teen years when our raging hormones demand that we explore the alluring world of sex. Sex is a built-in motive we lust after to satisfy our ardent curiosity as well as our growing physiological needs.

We have all been there.

The first guy I had sex with had an insatiable sex drive. He was more experienced than me but once we started, it was on for young and old — anywhere, anytime. It didn't matter where we were or who was around, there was a time when his hand became an almost permanent addition in my panties.

Hmm … maybe that's where my love of fingers originated. He did have skill in the finger department, but that's about where it ended.

Our relationship lasted for 5 years before we called it quits. He thought that he'd be able to come back and marry me some future day when he was ready. I thought otherwise, and it had nothing to do with the fact that although we had been highly active in the bedroom, he wasn't a great lover.

Why?

It's like the million-dollar question for women everywhere. We can never quite tell for sure if a man is going to be great in the sack until we're actually rolling in it with him. I mean, every man knows the basics — give her a smooch; fondle her here; rub there; part her thighs and hammer in. But that's just sex.

Any guy can sex it up but that doesn't make him an unforgettable lover.

Personally, I feel as if the tell-tale signs of a man's sexual prowess may be prevalent through his developed tastes, level of creativity and small nuances outside of the bedroom.

Men who have a creative side and practice extracurricular activities are usually more broad-minded, soulful and more in tune with their senses and with life. As are those men who are spontaneous and adventurous — who are not uptight or feel the need to schedule every minute of every day. Guys with these types of characteristics tend to show up in the bedroom and make for better lovers.

My ex-boyfriend was all about the visual senses and fast-action and less about exploring and developing sensual pleasures and savouring my body. His arousal was defined by handling me as if I was his sex-toy — here to serve and please his desires with little regard for my own. He enjoyed my body, but only to the extent his primitive style of passion allowed. In other words, he was never interested in refining his skills as a lover — and no, he didn't possess a creative flair or a deep passion to experience life in new ways.

He was rather humdrum, really.

Not every man or woman is actually interested in taking the time to learn how to be a great lover, opting instead to remain a lousy lay and/or continue to see sex as a means to an end — a quick orgasmic release or an act carried out for the purpose of pro-creation.

Both viewpoints are kind of dull if you ask me. Imagine if we only had sex to procreate?

Frustration. Overload.

We are sexually driven creatures by nature and the fact is that sex is one of the greatest aspects of our humanity. Anyone who has experienced orgasmic heaven and real connection with an attentive lover can attest to that.

Sex is pleasurable and fun; it helps to relieve stress

and strengthens our relationships and connections — it is the ultimate expression of love.

Speaking of expressions of love, here's a few ultimate traits that I consider vital in making a man an unforgettable lover — he has:

Lips Like Seduction

Kissing can be totally amazing or … erm … worthy of a good cringe followed by a fast excuse to bail out.

The way a man kisses a woman is a huge indication of his underlying passion to connect deeply — and deep connection is what makes an unforgettable lover.

But please don't throw in the towel too early. We all know that first kiss can be a little nerve-wracking and less-than-perfect what with the pressure and all — but if it begins to heat up and gets you all bothered, then pay attention, girl — you may have a Casanova on your hands!

An unforgettable lover knows how to use his lips like a seductive art form to induce a rush of deep arousal in his woman; and he enjoys every moment of building the sexual tension through his kiss.

Passion Like Fever

Love is the most important element in a relationship and passion is the fire that helps to create total fusion. There must exist an intense sexual desire for your partner and a deep need to express strong emotion through love-making to reach the next level in intimacy.

Sometimes, the only way to channel and express our

emotions in totality is through the act of sex. Like an outlet for our deepest and most sacred parts. We cannot always fully articulate the depth of our feelings to the person we love — so, when words are not enough we use our bodies; bonding through our passion can convey infinitely loving feelings.

An unforgettable lover possesses and expresses his feelings in his lover's touch — he isn't afraid to show his love for his woman through acts of unbridled passion.

Attentiveness Like Arousal

The most unforgettable lovers are the ones who are in tune with their woman and are attentive to her needs and desires in the bedroom.

Forget the 5-minute wham-bam. There will be no thank you, ma'am's from this side of the bed. A man who is an unforgettable lover knows the importance of pacing; he's the real chill-deal who relishes sweet sensations and sensual caresses, and he will take his cues from his woman — her pleasure is his greatest turn-on.

Psychology Today: "One of women's main sexual complaints about their lovers is that men rush into intercourse before women feel ready for genital play."

I can't tell you how many times my lady friends have expressed the very same thing — slow down and then get a little slower.

An unforgettable lover considers his lover's entire body his erotic playground and savours every inch — he knows how to prime her for the main event.

But not before a little…

Tongue Like Erotica

It would be impossible to not add the fine and delicate art of cunnilingus to a list of traits constituting an unforgettable lover. He must honor the pussy who he seeks to take and if he can't or won't give her the gift of his passionate kiss in her most intimate parts, then all cards are off the table.

More than just eating pussy; it's a constitution that requires developed skill and intentional attention to tap into and connect with his woman's essence via his lips and tongue.

An unforgettable lover has a strong desire to know his woman's body and learn what turns her on. He wants to taste her sex — he knows that her scent is all his and he'll push her to the edge of desire — allowing her to linger in the throes of erotica, lust and love as he ignites her inner-Sex Goddess.

$\sim$

An unforgettable lover is a man who has passion, patience and a deep sense of appreciation for love, connection and all of life. He is open to experiencing moments of vulnerability and probably has a delightful kinky side, too; but most importantly, he sees sex for what it really is — a gift.

A beautiful, beautiful gift.

3

DANCING WITH THE DEVIL: HOW TO COMBAT EMOTIONAL AND PSYCHOLOGICAL MANIPULATORS

*I*t sounds rather dramatic, doesn't it - to dance with the devil?

The thought instantly conjures grotesque visions and disturbing swirls in the pit of your stomach. Well, it should, anyhow. I mean, the devil is a personification of everything evil and sinister. Portrayed as a dark enigmatic beast, he is seen as the manifestation of wicked - an objectification of a hostile and destructive force.

The concept of the devil is entwined throughout our history, mythology, art and literature. He is known by many names like Satan, Beelzebub, Mephistopheles and Lucifer. He has been known to possess souls and seduce humans, and has become a fascinating and popular supernatural character on our screens.

But Is he real?

Pope Francis says: *"The Devil is more intelligent than*

mere mortals and should never be argued with - he is evil, he's not like mist. He's not a diffuse thing, he is a person."

Total disclosure – I am not a religious person. This post isn't about religion nor do I wish argue the complexities surrounding faith and denomination. I wasn't raised to adhere to any religious deity, but that doesn't make me any less aware of the deplorable acts capable by mankind.

Where there is light, so there is darkness.

Sometimes, that dark force can be found in people. It is unfortunate, but true. We have seen the effects of darkness occur through our history, and continue to witness it today with large scale conflict and wars, inequality and corruption.

Yet, it is the vicious acts playing out between us at an intimate level that have the ability to really cut deep. Some people are extremely skilled at psychological manipulation. Moreover, they seem to gain some kind of twisted satisfaction from doing so.

Whether we refer to these people as the "devil-in-action" or sociopaths makes little difference in the scheme of things, because once you have become their target, you'd better pick up your game quick smart or you risk losing your mind.

These people have no sense of empathy or compassion; and as you will discover as we get further into this post, nor do they take responsibility for the harm they cause - enter the emotional or psychological manipulator.

~

"He's more intelligent than us, and he'll turn you upside down; he'll make your head spin"

- Pope Francis - on the devil.

Did you ever find yourself caught in a twisted mind-game you never saw coming until it was too late and your head was spinning?

I have.

Emotional or psychological manipulators often use mind games to seize power in a relationship. The ultimate goal is to use that power to control the other person.

These people will use an array of weapons to accomplish their goal. These techniques can include sneaky, deceptive or underhanded tactics to change the thinking, behavior, or perceptions of their victim.

It is no secret that a healthy relationship is based on trust, understanding, and mutual respect. This is true of personal relationships as well as professional ones. Sometimes, people seek to exploit these elements of a relationship in order to benefit themselves in some way.

Sometimes, we find ourselves waltzing with the devil.

The signs of emotional and psychological manipulation can be subtle. They are often hard to identify, especially when it is happening to you and particularly when you are emotionally invested in someone.

We all know how it feels to be in love, but what happens when that special someone deliberately sets out to exploit your feelings?

It can feel as if you are fighting to tread water while the sea slowly sucks your soul and your heart withers.

Hollow hope - that is one sure-fire sign you've got an emotional or psychological manipulator on your hands. They are masters at stringing you along by the threads of your heart while offering smidgens of false hope in an underhanded manner.

In fact, they are masters at quite a few psychological tricks. In order to identify whether you have encountered or are in the process of "dancing with a devil", it is important to familiarize yourself with the tactics these people use so you can avoid falling victim to their games.

Let's flush out some of the tell-tale signs.

According to psychology author George K. Simon, some of the signs and techniques used by an emotional or psychological manipulator are:

- Concealing aggressive intentions and behaviors while appearing affable.
- Knowing the psychological vulnerabilities of

the victim to determine which tactics are likely to be the most effective.

- Having a sufficient level of ruthlessness to have no qualms about causing harm to the victim if necessary.
- Lying by omission: This is a subtle form of lying by withholding a significant amount of the truth. This technique is also used in propaganda.
- Denial: The manipulator refuses to admit that they have done something wrong or have taken part in causing the situation to evolve.
- Rationalization: An excuse made by the manipulator for inappropriate behavior.
- Minimization: This is a type of denial coupled with rationalization. The manipulator asserts that their behavior is not as harmful or irresponsible as someone else is suggesting.
- Shaming: The manipulator uses sarcasm and put-downs to increase fear and self-doubt in the victim. Manipulators use this tactic to make others feel unworthy and therefore defer to them. They can make one feel ashamed for even daring to challenge them. It is an effective way to foster a sense of inadequacy in the victim.
- Playing the victim role: A manipulator portrays themselves as a victim of

circumstance or of someone else's behavior in order to gain pity, sympathy or evoke compassion from another.

- Projecting the blame: Manipulators will claim that the victim is the one who is at fault for believing lies that they were conned into believing, as if the victim forced the manipulator to be deceitful. It is frequently used as a means of psychological and emotional manipulation and control.

These are just some of the tactics used by emotional and psychological manipulators. The effect of their behavior can have detrimental and devastating consequences to their victims – if we allow them to hold that power.

"Never be bullied into silence. Never allow yourself to be made a victim. Accept no one's definition of your life, but define yourself."

- Harvey Fierstein

Experiencing the manipulating behavior of someone who uses your emotions as their punching bag is like walking between night and day. Sometimes, it feels as if you are in heaven; as if the sun is shining just for you.

Other times, it feels as if you are dodging a suspended sword waiting to strike for the kill. And then it does; and the devil reveals himself and you feel as if are the most foolish person to wander the murky path existing between night and day.

Sometimes, people set out to hurt others with malicious intent.

It may take time to realize when someone is emotionally manipulating you. The signs are so subtle and underhanded in nature, and they often evolve over time. If you think you are being treated in this way, it is important to trust your instincts and believe in yourself.

You are not powerless; you can do something about it.

You can take back your personal power and know your worth. Respect, love and dignity – you are worth all of these and more. You are worth more than what your emotional manipulator will have you believe.

Apologize for your part and move on.

Often, there is a complexity of emotional entanglement existing between an emotional manipulator and their victim. Each action causes a reaction; we are fooling ourselves if we believe we don't have an effect on people. High-level situations induce high-level reactions that may find you behaving in ways that baffle you.

Don't try to beat them.

Two people should not play this game – the stakes are high when it comes to the heart. Instead, learn to recognize the strategies so you can properly prepare your responses.

Set boundaries.

When an emotional or psychological manipulator realizes they are losing control, their tactics may grow more desperate. They may lash out and falsely accuse you of wrongful behavior to induce a sense of shame and/or delusion, or make outrageous threats based on fabrications.

This is the time for you to make some difficult decisions.

You do not have to have this person in your life. You have a choice. You can choose to comply to the person in control or you can be proactive - you can cut them from your life.

This may be a great time to recruit support in the form of trusted friends or a therapist. Gaining insight from an individual outside of the situation can help to find clarity.

Learn your lessons.

You can heal and grow from this. Keep positive. No one deserves to have another individual treat them in this manner. Emotional and psychological manipulation may not leave physical scars, but it can have a long-lasting effect – especially when you opened your heart to someone who abused it.

Even when somebody you love turns out to be the "devil", it is vital to remember that love is never lost or wasted in this world. If you loved, then you didn't lose. Sometimes, we have to dance with the devil in order to see the light - and it shines bright for you.

4

LONG-DISTANCE SEX, LIES AND WEBCAM

"You've got the best pussy I've ever seen."
"Erm ... thanks."

Even if it wasn't the truth, it had to be a good thing. After all, said "pussy" had pushed out three healthy-sized babies. I'm talking over eight-pound deliveries here. Yes, flinch if you must. I did. In the most severe way possible.

Of course, we should not actually utter the word "pussy" and "baby" (as in birthing one) in the same sentence. To do so can almost be considered a cardinal sin.

You knew that, right? Obviously, a vagina gives birth and *not* a pussy.

A pussy is for fun and pleasure – she's that dark sultry number in a short sprayed-on black dress parading her assets with a sign on her well-rounded ass saying "open for business". Or she's that bouncy blonde who teases and tantalizes; fluttering long lashes in just the right way while sporting thighs hard enough to strangle a giant armadillo.

Yeah. She's like an Amazon native goddess with legs that never end. Legs, that when parted actually do reveal the best pussy you've ever seen.

Her vagina hasn't stretched to the size of a giant armadillo yet, and she certainly hasn't spent an hour trying not to think about the hot doctor peering between her legs as if solving the puzzle of the century. Needle and thread in hand. Casually talking about last night's dinner and movie with the assisting nurse.

Newsflash – it matters not how hot or sexy a woman appears, or how bright that sign illuminates on her ass as she saunters across the room, at some point, her pussy will become a vagina.

And that vagina is always open for business. Just not in the pleasure-inducing sex kind of way. A vagina encompasses all that gritty, womanly stuff that most men don't like to think about.

It bleeds; it stretches to become a birth canal; it is subjected to all kinds of medical tools (some of these are sharp – see above); it discharges and aches; it endures hot wax and razors; and sometimes, it becomes home to unwanted blemishes in the form of ingrown hairs.

Ouch.

How sexy is the pussy sounding now?

'It was like watching my favorite pub burn down."

Those words were spoken by a man I know (and won't name) after he had witnessed the birth of his first child.

Uh-oh. He watched his pussy become an actual vagina. Perhaps a few sessions of therapy are in need to help fix the mental-scarring and foster his path into becoming a real man. You know, the kind who typically don't view women as sexual objects. These are the same kind of men who can handle a woman so well, that they don't make a distinction between a vagina and a pussy.

They honor the vagina.

Honestly, given that there are men out there who liken the birthing process as pussy-devastation (of the nation), I should be grateful that my charred coochie was given the upmost of compliments (see opening quote). Although, I must confess that the words were dished out over thousands of miles separating us and through the lens of a camera.

We all know everything appears better through webcam, right? Just ask my mother.

Wait – *whaat?*

Okay, I'm stopping you right there. I am quite certain that my mother hasn't seen my vagina since I finished potty training. You're twisted if you even began to venture down that road.

But each time she views one of my weekly CWE

podcast videos on YouTube, I'm confronted by conversations that go something like this:

"How do you do that?"

"Do what?"

"Look like that on video?"

"Huh?"

"Your skin looks so smooth ... I want some of that. You must have great make-up."

"Erm ... thanks, ma."

That was a sarcastic thanks, by the way.

In any case, I haven't flashed my gash on webcam for over a decade now, and when I was getting it on with my cam-lover, I didn't apply make-up to my nether regions either.

Which brings me to ... pussy-cam, anyone? How about a little cock-cam to fill in your monitor on a cold and lonely night?

I am not talking about online porn. This is much sexier, much more intimate and a gazillion times more erotic.

Before you begin to squirm and get uncomfortable at the thought of getting sexy with a cam-lover, think about how the brain plays such a powerful part when it comes to sex.

A wealth of scientific research establishes the brain's primary role in sexual activity. That's why sexually driven language is so arousing - couple that with a camera and someone you trust, and the desire to engage in cam-sex becomes almost impossible to ignore.

In short, cam-sex is obscenely erotic and exceptionally spicy. Added bonus: experiencing sex in this way can benefit a long-distance relationship.

When your lover resides on the other side of the world, sex across the web can be especially sensual – it helps to keep the frustration in check between the long months spent apart. It also helps to nurture the intimacy between you and strengthen vital relationship elements such as trust, respect and communication; it deepens the bonds with your lover.

Long-distance relationships are extremely challenging to maintain. No one ever claimed it was going to be easy. In fact, your friends are likely to tell you how crazy you are for even considering it.

Mine did. The thing is, when somebody captures your heart, it is amazing how circumstances and obstacles seem to fade into the "it'll be okay" pile in the back of your mind. Love does that to people – it takes away the impossibilities until you're left with faith.

Still, it takes a copious amount of effort and trust to make a long-distance relationship work. The extra space between you makes many things unachievable. Things could get complicated, and you could get sad and lonely at times.

Long-distance relationships may be tough but they have their own sweet surprises too. It is important to be clear with what each of you want and expect from the union – and just as vital to make the time for each other.

We played online games, listened to music and surfed the net together. We watched clips and movies, and spent hours exchanging titbits about our cultural differences. But when it came to keeping our love alive and strong, it was time for a little long-distance loving via a webcam.

Creative thinking is crucial if you want the relationship to succeed. Getting saucy and naughty over the web can help with relieving some of the tension and strain that builds in these kinds of scenarios; and it all begins with a little bit of the dirty language.

Robert Montenegro from Big Think says:

"Dirty talk feeds our need for intimate conversation and lust for sexual activity. It provides a multi-layered sexual experience that extends further than just physical touch. Dirty talk works because it's sex through suggestion, and to our brains, suggestion can be just as powerful as full-on execution."

Damned straight. If you ask me, it's the suggestive hints and sexy inuendo that really gets temperatures soaring toward the risqué.

While getting indecent with words holds much delight, dirty talk eventually escalates into using more visual means of communication. All good. There is something extremely provocative when you're alone with your vibrator, a camera and watching the way your lover's eyes darken before he … explodes on screen.

There is also something intensely stimulating when someone tells you what they want to see you do next. And you do it.

Groan.

Break out the lingerie and really work the fun; eBay is a friend.

I loaded up on lacy teddies, crotchless panties and an extremely improper naughty nurse piece. I even snagged an especially sexy festive piece just for Christmas. Whips, cuffs and dildos didn't go astray when getting fun and creative with the online kink sessions, either. All of which he appreciated.

Look, no couple can be in a long-distance relationship forever. It is super important that you're both on the same page. Make a plan; a time-line estimating the time spent apart and the time you can be together as you work toward a shared vision – a life with your significant other.

It helps to view the experience as a journey.

"Real gold is not afraid of the test of fire."

- An old Chinese byword.

If each situation and relationship we encounter throughout our lifetimes is really a personal lesson designed to help us evolve, then the long-distance relationship has to be one of the most testing to endure.

This is when we discover love in an entirely new way, as well as learn just far we are willing to go for love. If the love is real, the experience can only bound you together even stronger.

The best thing about spicing up a long-distance relationship is that sweet moment when you are finally together again. They are the same moments that you're thankful of the time and energy invested into the relationship; that you saw the worth in pushing through the hard times and persevering when hopelessness and loneliness rimmed and you toyed with giving it all up.

They also become the moments when you get to use all those raunchy pieces and sex toys together. My Canadian guy loved it when I played naughty-nurse in the real world. And I loved it each time he exploded within arm's reach.

He happened to love my vagina too.

5

IS ALL FAIR IN LOVE AND WAR?

*M*y mother was severely abused as a child. She is a twin. Her sister was born first. Then, it became apparent there was another baby – my mother.

It was during the late 1940's, a time when determining a twin pregnancy wasn't as easy as it is today. My grandmother already had two little ones to care for and was expecting to birth one more child and not two.

She instantly rejected my mother.

After her hospital stay, my grandmother returned home with the twins, and despite her husband's protests, she gave her newborn baby away to their neighbors. She wanted nothing to do with the second born twin.

My mother was fortunate that the neighbors were

lovely people. The couple took her in and cared for her as if one of their own. With them, she found security and love. She was cuddled, touched and encouraged. Her needs were met in every way that a newborn baby requires in order to thrive and grow mentally and emotionally.

She remained with them for the first two years of her life. Then, at the insistence of my grandfather, she eventually returned to live with her biological family. Her short life would never again be the same.

She was the unwanted child.

Love was replaced with hatred. Nurturing became neglect. Security was a fading memory in a two-year old's world as her mother set about stripping her of worthiness and virtue.

She did this through unthinkable acts of brutality and torture. She did this through inhumane treatment and emotional abuse. Think David James Pelzer and his story, *A Child Called It*, and you're on the right track.

I cannot imagine the state of internal crisis for a mother to treat her child with such cruelty. I can only assume that a soul must be so damaged and confused to have the ability to inflict such severe torment and suffering upon her own child.

My mum has often said how she wished her parents had left her with the neighbors. Those first two years of her life had somehow imprinted upon her soul and impressed in her memory. The fleeting time spent with that family proved to be vital in forming the fabric of her psyche and the breadth of her heart.

She had never forgotten what it felt like to be loved and nurtured.

I knew my grandmother before she died an early death, but my mother kept us away for the most part. She was a woman plagued with darkness. As you can imagine, she held little interest in me. Our relationship was nil to nothing and she had a way of scaring the bejesus out of me.

Every now and then, I look at old photos of the woman who abused my mother. Pictures of her with my grandfather when they were young. She had been a stunningly beautiful woman with soft, delicate features and lustrous dark hair.

The couple posed with grandeur - he in a classy black suit, while her petite figure was wrapped in white fur. They appeared sound in the knowledge of the path ahead of them; a future filled with promising visions and love. She's like a different woman in those pictures; a woman I never knew.

I realized that at one point in her life she had known happiness. She had known love.

So, what went wrong?

Life was vastly different back then. My grandfather was enlisted to serve in World War II at the age of twenty. He was ranked Private and became a prisoner of war in one of the most notorious of Japanese war camps: Changi prison.

He spent years being tortured in that prison along with thousands of other Australian men, including war hero, Sir Ernest Edward "Weary" Dunlop, who was my grandfather's friend.

James Saunderson was like a gentle giant. He was funny and charming; an ordinary Aussie kid ready to take on the world with his woman by his side. Until years of war, torture, death and imprisonment stole his light.

He never returned home the same. Those years haunted him. They were the same years that would snatch the light inside of my grandmother and prove the catalyst in my mother's mistreatment.

When life squeezes us, what comes out is what's on the inside.

It's one of the great lessons of life.

Living through war might be a radical example to use when discussing relationships. My grandfather's experience had devasting affects on his psyche that lasted through his lifetime. He spent years receiving psychiatric treatment; years suddenly erupting into violent bouts of rage.

The war took more than just my grandfather's mental health. It claimed my grandmother's quality of life, her dreams and her humanity. The war collected both of their soul's and darkened the lives of their children.

Did they have a choice?

We can never erase the past. We may never quite be able to take away the pain, but we can take measures to heal ourselves and work through the inner-demons to find the light again. In each moment, we have a choice.

When the pressure is on and out of you comes anything other than love, it is because that's what you've allowed to be inside. To live a highly functioning life, you need take away all those negative things you don't want in your life and replace them with love.

My mother is proof of this.

She could have easily embraced the mindset offered by her violent upbringing. She could have chosen bitterness and hatred, and carried the abuse through the generations, but she didn't.

Does the past still haunt her? It probably does sometimes. Yet, she has only ever spoken of her parents from the highest regard. Somehow, that little girl who was never shown the love she craved from her mother, grew up with the ability to accept the life she was handed and forgive her parents for every indiscretion.

She chooses to view them through the eyes of love and empathy – and this is a choice we all have regardless of how someone might upset or offend us, or whatever the situation confronting us.

All my mother had ever wanted was the love of her mother. Even on her death bed, my grandmother refused to convey the words she couldn't give.

My mum has lived her entire life without hearing her

own mother speak of her love for her, but every day I hope that I have enough inside of me to make up for the love denied her.

Although, I'm not sure that that will ever be enough to fill the void left in a little girl by a mother who couldn't find a way to snatch back her light and open her heart.

6

DEATH LESSONS: OVERCOMING THE FEAR OF DEATH

*T*he only certainty we face is death.

Sounds a bit morbid and frightening, but it doesn't need to be. Let me explain.

Death is the ultimate reminder of our mortality. It's inevitable and mysterious territory, and sometimes it can strike without warning. We can never really be sure when death will claim us or a loved one. With all the unsettling fears that might grip us about death, that one is probably the most disturbing.

Death should have its own soul.

Wayne Dyer once said:

"Change the way you look at things, and the things you look at change."

I have talked about this quote on more than one occasion because I know firsthand the power of those words. By fusing my thoughts and immersing myself with the meaning of that simple phrase, I've been able to transform seemingly immovable situations, as well as the relationships in my life.

The same is true when it comes to fearing death.

But it isn't until we experience the death of someone close that we realize how important it is to relish our time here on earth and cherish the relationships bound to transform form us along the way. Most of all, though, it is when we begin to contemplate and feel our sacred connection to the universe that we sense our *immortality.*

I used to be afraid of death. When I was a child, the thought of losing a parent crippled me on the inside. Then, when I became a parent, it was contemplating the death of one of my children that proved too much to bear.

Nowadays, I deliberately steer my thoughts away from such notions – worrying about circumstances beyond my control is useless. I know this at an intellectual and soul level. Yet, I am far from perfect. My over-active brain doesn't always acquiesce to this knowledge.

Through my late teenage years and into my early 20's, I spent a lot of time at my boyfriend's house, staying there most nights of the week.

Danny is the boy who owns a lot my "firsts", including my first experience in a long-term relationship. He was the first boy who ever loved me romantically and the first I'd slept with. More than that, he was the first boy to show me what it meant when someone else cared.

He stole my heart with his cheeky grin, fast lip and long dark lashes.

He made me laugh.

During the early years, Danny was full of life and ever the boy vying for his father's approval. He was great with his hands and possessed a sharp mind. He taught me to drive a car and a speedboat, and patiently coached me how water-ski.

He introduced me to culinary delights like lobster mornay, and we spent hours burning up endless highways while listening to music during interstate road trips.

His family became my family. Literally. My mother went on to marry his father. Which technically transformed my boyfriend into my step-brother.

Meh. Life is weird like that.

As it turned out, our relationship didn't last as long as our folks' marriage. For all the great qualities Danny possessed, there was an extreme flip-side to his personality; a darkness that lingered on sadistic and a craving for addiction that would be his undoing.

Danny is dead now.

His mother used to tell me she believed that when you die there is nothing else. That this was it – this one lifetime here in the now.

One life. One chance.

Thousands of conversations and thoughts had passed between us during those years, and these are the words that have stayed with me. Even then, I found it difficult to believe in her convictions.

I couldn't accept that death was final.

Danny used to tell me that to play *"In the Air Tonight"* by Phil Collins at any less than full volume was a crime. He used to say that I was the love of his life and that someday, he was going to marry me.

That never happened. His desire to quench his growing addictions led him down a path that I rejected. The boy I fell in love with and thought I knew had chosen a journey that had shocked me.

He chose heroin.

Twenty years of silence had passed between us when I learned of Danny's death. Still, during his final days he spoke of me and the love he still kept for me. He had told his sister that I remained his greatest love, despite my absence from his life.

He was just forty-two years old.

I am a deep thinker. This quality has been particular to me ever since I can remember. As a small child, I spent hours observing my family and noticing their divinity – peering past the flesh until their physicality felt foreign to me. The same holds true when staring at my own reflection.

Of course, I was too young to have the correct terminology in my knowledge data base to vocalize what I was experiencing, or indeed to even string together a prolonged chain of coherent thoughts about the subject.

Besides, if I had voiced to my parents what I was actually thinking, they probably would've pinned me as "special" before thumbing through the phone directory for a local children's shrink.

Heh. What *was* I thinking? And how does this relate to death?

Stay with me.

I was thinking the thoughts of every five-year-old, of course.

Who am I? What I am doing in this body? This isn't me. That isn't really them. How did we even get here?

I felt like an imposter in my own body. It sounds weird, I know.

Have you ever become super silent, stood before your reflection and really looked deep into yourself? Something happens when you peer past your flesh – you get a glimpse at your soul and sense your divinity.

The *immortal* part of you.

When you come to sense that truth, the fearful thoughts surrounding death lessens as you realize that death does not equate with finality. It exists as a transition into a dimension that is more real than the fleeting life we experience here on the earth-plane.

The day Danny died I had distinctly felt his energy pass through me. I became aware of his presence and his love. It felt tranquil, humbling and positive. A few hours later and in my car running an errand, I tuned into the radio to catch the beginning of *In the Air Tonight.*

The wave of emotion was incredible. He wasn't gone. He is all around and sees everything.

We can't always explain the strange synchronicities and phenomena that takes place in our world, but that doesn't mean it doesn't exist. To close your mind from the greater aspects of life, death and love, and judge those that are able to embrace the unknown is a disservice to your soul.

Death does have a soul.

It is through death that I have learned that once the embers of love ignite, they cannot cease to exist. Love really does transcend time and space.

Death's soul showed me the importance of graciousness, humility and respect, and how vital it is that we practice these qualities in every situation we encounter; as well as every action and reaction we chose for ourselves.

Death drove home the gravity of compassion and gratitude.

Thinking beyond my physicality and questioning my existence eventually stretched my perspective to instil a sense of self and belonging – an affinity to something greater than myself. That realm that holds the most sacred part of us and connects us to everything; the universal consciousness.

It was death that showed me what it means to be alive by giving me a sense of inner-freedom.

7

THE MOST IMPORTANT RELATIONSHIP OF YOUR LIFE

We never stop learning through our relationships with people. Or rather, people never stop teaching us. It has taken a long time for me to learn how to trust my intuition. It's been a journey paved with dark nights of the soul, as well as amazing moments of clarity.

Throughout my earlier years, I had always doubted my inner-gut feelings or just plain ignored them. I never quite trusted myself — or who I was, for that matter.

One prime example was when my first husband proposed to me. It wasn't that I didn't love him. It was more that I was just twenty-one years old and reasonably fresh out of a five-year relationship. I had plans. I was working to save money for travel. New York beckoned me with a pull I couldn't deny.

He took me to the beach, produced a diamond and

spoke words that would claim me. I'll never forget that day. Not because it was the happiest day of my life or anything — it is more the distinct memory of ignoring the inner-turmoil circling through my head as I accepted the ring and said "yes".

The inner-screams were yelling "no", by the way.

His blue eyes were so vulnerable as he looked at me expectantly. I didn't have the heart to turn him down, despite that marriage wasn't on my agenda at that time.

You can call it gutless. You can even call it stupid. Maybe a bit of both?

I used to be a soft touch. I think I still might be. Better that than a heartless human. Like some.

Fact: When you ignore your intuition, shit will probably hit the fan. The lessons will be harder.

It wasn't even that marriage would deny me the freedom of travel. It was that that marriage became a living nightmare. As it turned out, his true qualities eventually surfaced to reveal a narcissistic and violent man.

I ignored my inner-warning bells and experienced great pain because of it.

One for the intuition.

People have screwed me over. I'm certain you've been screwed over, too. It happens to be a part of this thing called life.

Years later and following the inevitable divorce (that wasn't gutless), a very handsome man asked me out for dinner. I was so nervous. It would be my first date with someone new in twelve years.

In the moments leading up to his arrival, I remember hitting rewind on Pearl Jam's *"Black"* over and over. It was my favorite. Yeah. I was into Pearl Jam (not as much as my friend who named her vibrator "Eddie"). Somehow, listening to that song quelled my nerves. Somewhat.

It was probably a sign from the Intuition Gods.

Was it normal to feel this uneasy before a date?

He played league cricket and had mutual sporting connections with one of my closet friends who had been a professional hockey player for the Australian team. And he was hot.

Bonus.

Still, I couldn't quite conquer the whirring sirens in the back of my mind. Something didn't feel right. I'd met him once. I didn't miss his dominant energy, but I did pretend not to notice.

He took me to dinner and followed up with a side of date-rape.

That didn't go down so well. Another one for intuition.

The next day, my girlfriend looked at me and said, "I hope this doesn't make you bitter — not all men are pricks."

Just some. I seemed to be a magnet for them.

Truth is, I knew that if I allowed others to infect my

outlook on life with their shit-ass, negative behavior, that would be letting them win. Unfortunately, some people do want to bring you down.

Fact: Even your intuition can get it wrong.

Wait — not really. Please don't start distrusting those gut feelings you've worked so hard to strengthen — they are designed to lead you along the right path and help you learn.

I think I've worked it out — it is all about the lessons. Remember my opening paragraph? These little lesson-nuggets are about helping us nurture our relationship with our inner-guidance.

Even when we get it wrong. In fact, sometimes we are supposed to get it wrong. Other times, we're not actually getting it wrong — it's the other person in question that isn't quite getting it.

Confused?

I don't blame you.

Take a soul connection for instance.

What? You didn't think I could get through a post about intuition without including a spiel about your soul?

It's the only real part of us, you realize …

Let's explore a little.

Have you ever met someone and instantly felt an indescribably strong connection toward them? It feels as if your soul recognizes them and your human part is tripping to catch up.

Soul connections are no mistake. They arrive in our

lives to trigger inner-growth and fuel creativity, as well as to create new patterns of love in the world and foster our path toward enlightenment. They show up to open new thought concepts and kick-start your heart.

They show up to blow your mind.

When these special people arrive on the scene, you cannot ignore the deep sensations the meeting ignites.

Rare gems. Real world.

That's right, I said "real world".

Ermm ... and what is "real"? I hear you ask.

Real is that which doesn't change. Your soul won't cark it. Your body will.

Don't be so hasty to dismiss what your physical senses cannot detect. You cannot see love but you know it exists because you feel it, right? Well, I hope you do. Real love doesn't change. You can't see your intuition either, by the way.

Speaking of intuition, all of that instinctual drive you've been cultivating over the years seems to fall to the wayside when encountering a significant soul connection. All for a purpose — to test and explode the boundaries of love while propelling you into greater states of awareness.

To learn to love unconditionally.

Fact: Meeting someone you know in soul isn't all peaches and cream.

Far from it, actually. It's not supposed to be. The true soul connection is designed to make you feel uncomfortable because its created to evoke fire to change. It's about pushing your inner-boundaries and shattering pre-existing beliefs and societal expectations on what is deemed as "acceptable".

We're good at doing that, you know — imposing systems of "right and wrongs", judging one another and acting from a place of fear. Which isn't real by the way.

Your soul wasn't created to fear. The human condition did that.

In short, a soul meeting of this nature will stretch your perspective beyond your physicality and catapult you into "trigger zone" while developing your inner-strength and self-belief. A realm reserved for facing yourself — the good and the not so good.

Sounds like a picnic, huh?

Growth is never easy. You will need to courage-up to get through this thing called life and actually grasp greater perspectives. *Free your mind*. Start by contemplating the real stuff.

Some people have what it takes to explore deep love. Others do not.

When you're there, you discover moments that will define you for the rest of your life — moments when you either choose take a leap of faith, or run back to your comfort zone screaming, *"Hell, no!"*

When confronted with matters of deep soul truths, it becomes more important than ever to lean on your inner-guidance system. It's as if each experience, relationship and past lesson have been in preparation for the ultimate test of faith. When trusting your intuition becomes vital.

My Shamanic Medicine Drumming Teacher often speaks of giving thanks to our paths. She reminds us that it is unique to each of us; that it stretches before us perfectly raw and unpaved; and that we shouldn't be afraid to be true to ourselves as we walk toward the unknown.

She instills the courage.

Sacred soul journeys are more about personal growth than the other person actually "getting it". It is when we learn how to open our hearts and free our minds that we begin to connect with our souls to live authentically.

And that is what its all about.

Life.

At the end of it all, it is through our soul connections and relationships that will result in refining our most important relationship of all — **the one you have with yourself.**

Self-discovery is there for the taking if you but have courage enough to wade through mysterious territory and trust the path.

One for me.

P.S. I did make it to New York. Right after my divorce.

8

THE ECSTASY OF SOUL SEX

*L*et's talk about sex. I don't mean the run-of-the-mill penetrative kind of sex that you're used to reading about and have probably been practicing for a good portion of your adult life.

I'm talking about unearthly pleasures, sensual indulgences and exquisite peaks that exist within the deeper dimensions of your psyche – essentially, sex without the ... erm ... sex part.

Soul sex.

Sound weird?

There was a time when the notion of soul sex would have instantly evoked an eyeroll. I would've dismissed it as some farfetched concept reserved for the delusional.

So, it is important to clear this up at the onset – I'm not writing this post out of a psychiatric hospital. Promise. I am not delusional, either. But something has occured between the time when I would have found soul sex difficult to fathom to arriving here, in this moment - I encountered somebody significant.

Someone connected in soul.

If you stripped away your flesh and blood, what or who do you think you would be?

Socrates said: *"That energy, or soul, is separate from matter and that the universe is made of energy – pure energy."*

Including us.

Take the atom for example – it's the basic building block for matter. Quantum physics tells us that as we go deeper and deeper into the workings of the atom, we discover that there is nothing there – just energy waves.

It says an atom is actually an invisible force field - a kind of miniature tornado which emits waves of electrical energy.

Energy.

In the realm of sexual energy, we are talking about a life-force energy that is fundamental to our humanity. It is through our sexual energy that we cultivate a relationship with desire, creativity and connectedness – not only to others but also to ourselves.

It is through our sexual energy that we learn how to own our perfectly flawed and sacred human bodies. But we are more than our human bodies. We are eternal beings experiencing a human life.

The soul is the ultimate lover.

Soul sex is much more than just an intermingling of sexual energy and desire. It is the process of becoming aware of a part of yourself that is deeply connected to another – emotionally, sexually, and spiritually, and then allowing them access to look into your soul.

Soul-merging is the ultimate act of vulnerability.

Making love in soul is the experience of completely opening yourself and surrendering to your partner. It is not unlike participating in a divine soul dance that becomes a fabric of who you are. Once your soul has recognized and united with its counterpart, you can never forget. Even if you wanted to.

This kind of love making doesn't feel like physical sex, yet it goes beyond any pleasure known in the physical form. It feels as if you are becoming one with all that is - a feeling of complete love, connection and bliss. Perfection.

Soul sex is timeless, spaceless and absolute; it is pure universal bliss.

Merging with your soul counterpart is the definition of true love, energetic healing and intimacy because you are mating with your eternal lover – you are blending with a part of yourself that you've known since you came into creation.

This is why there is an element of healing that accompanies this sexual experience. Through fusing in soul with your significant other, you are essentially connecting with the love of source energy. It's like therapy for the heart and soul.

When you allow someone access to your soul, you are granting them permission to precious places and buried secrets within you. You are allowing them to:

- See and feel you in soul.
- Hear your soul voice.
- Touch, caress and entangle your soul with their own.
- Sense your smell.
- Invade and own your heart.
- Know, taste and excite you in soul.
- Kiss and make love to your soul.
- Experience you through intricate and personal pathways.
- Love you in your entirety.

Granting this level of access to someone is a gift to each of you, and should be treated with the utmost of respect and privilege at all times. Unfortunately, knowing someone in soul doesn't always equate with their outer personality and behavior.

The soul is eternally perfect. Humans are beautifully flawed.

A cautionary word.

When you encounter a person and sense their significance to you in soul, it is natural to become excited

- but it's worth stepping back to assess the situation and your soul counterpart in his human personality before investing emotionally, as these divine connections have the ability to trigger all kinds of pain and mayhem. Despite the divinity surrounding the bond.

However, once the connection ignites and you have experienced fusion at the soul level, change is inevitable. This is when you realize that no other relationship or sexual encounter before was ever deep enough. That no other love compared, nor did it quench the thirst for the deep level and transcendental loving that you never knew existed.

Until now.

If handled authentically, true soul sex can only deepen as the connection deepens. It is an endless relationship made for continual discovery, self-growth and exploration; and it will be the purest love you've ever had the privilege to experience here on earth.

If you honor it.

9

LOVE OR FEAR — YOU GET TO CHOOSE EVERY TIME

*W*hen I was fifteen years old, one of my friends decided to hate me. I had known her since Kindergarten and we had been close. I'd spent so much time at her house that her family was an extension of my own. Including her pudgy Golden Retriever, Candy-girl, who shared a mutual adoration with me.

Kids can be fickle when it comes to friendship. I'd experienced my fair share of "friends with conditions", but not within this relationship. She was special. I loved her and I had thought she loved me back. When her friendship turned into hostility, it shocked me to my foundations.

More than that, though, I was hurt beyond measure. My world suddenly blackened with an indescribable pain because not only had she turned against me; she was also in a position of power to influence all of my other friends in joining her on the "Hate Kim" bandwagon.

None of them knew why I was suddenly branded an outcast — there was no reason behind her animosity. **Yet, they all fell into place like puppets on a string.** One former friend was even commissioned by their "leader" to physically attack me. I was never one of those tough girls that went around looking for a fight.

Neither was my opponent.

She went ahead and did it anyway. She hit me and I hit her back. It wasn't long before we were surrounded by a horde of hollering teenagers as we attempted to ... god knows what because neither of us could actually fight.

When a teacher came along to break it up, I remember one of the "tough" girls sniggering the obvious as we were carted off to the Principal's office.

"You guys can't fight for shit."

Yeah. No *shit*, Sherlock.

Cue Michael Jackson: *I think I told you, I'm a lover not a fighter.*

Kylie and I were stuffed into the same waiting room outside the Principal's office and promptly left alone. We looked at each other. I took in her busted lip and noted the aches reverberating around my own body. I was shaken and upset, and knew that I ought to be feeling angry and outraged for the disgusting treatment handed to me by my peers.

Yet, I couldn't. All I saw was the expression in her eyes as they teared up and she said sorry.

Sorry.

There is power in that word. When expressed sincerely, a simple apology is all it takes to begin the path toward healing. Yet, an apology is easily negated if left unreceived.

The act of forgiveness is where true power lies.

I nodded.

"Okay."

It wasn't even a choice. I had forgiven her the moment she had caused me pain because I knew she acted out of fear and not malicious intent. A weight had lifted. We hugged before proceeding into the Principal's lair to receive our punishment.

Neville Goddard:

"The drama of life is a psychological one in which all the conditions, circumstances and events of your life are brought to pass by your assumptions."

In other words, your life path is determined by the feelings you assume. Focus on negative feelings like jealousy, hate and resentment, then you will discover your reality tainted by situations that evoke more of those feelings.

Steer your thoughts and focus toward the positive aspects of life and these feelings and experiences will become the dominant theme in your world.

Skeptical?

Pay close attention to those folks that fill in endless hours switching between the latest news channels. I'm willing to bet that they are among the biggest complainers in your life.

Each time you choose to watch a show, a movie or listen to a broadcast, you are making the choice to allow the essence of that broadcast into your personal energy field — you're effectively inviting the substance of that transmission into your life; which in turn evokes a deep reaction.

A feeling is assumed.

Keep watching or listening to something or someone who brings you down, that's where you'll find yourself. In a bottomless pit of self-repugnance and unrealized dreams.

The same holds true of people and the way we choose to treat one another.

I could have easily chosen to hold a grudge against Kylie for attacking me. In fact, most girls that age would have done just that. But gathering grudges and lashing out does nothing but wither your soul and hinder self-growth.

Deep down, you know this; each time you mistreat, disrespect or devalue another human being, there exists a tiny ping in the pit your gut that you might try to ignore — guilt. You cannot escape it. No matter how deep you bury it.

Don't make amends, it'll eventually catch up to you

one way or another. It always does. Life is designed this way — what you dish out is what you get back. In this life or the next...

As my mother likes to say: *It ain't over till the fat lady sings.*

It's never really over by the way. Nor is that my mother's quote, but I think you knew that.

People are always going to "broadcast" their message to influence your life or decisions in some way. Unfortunately, a lot of the time those people have their own interests and agendas at heart. Even when we think they are a friend.

Empathy is a resource that most of us are unwilling to invest for too many people. Sure, we're good at shooting off at the mouth about it. Putting it into practice is another matter altogether. It takes time and effort to understand how and why others feel the way they do. Even when motivated, doing so isn't always easy.

Without empathy, our relationships cease to exist. At least on any level worth experiencing. Yet, in those quiet moments when you're alone and the truth is staring you in the face, no amount of empathy or understanding from others can fill the void in your heart left by the choices you make.

The fact is, we were not born into this life to acquiesce to others. We came here to create our most fulfilling life; to make authentic connections, learn how to express love and value those that imprint upon our lives and souls along the way.

We came here to find freedom, joy and light in a condition of human struggle. We came to sift through it all to arrive at the place where we realize who we really are.

So, who are you?

It all begins by mastering our assumptions, how we treat others and how we choose to move through our ever-changing world. The way you see the world is how you will experience the world.

Love or fear?

That's the basic principle governing everything we encounter. It is love or fear that we choose to allow into our inner-worlds and will influence our life-energy, desires and outcomes.

Every time.

No one can choose for you. Nobody knows what or who is best for you except you.

Friends, acquaintances and family — they all have their own unique paths and they don't own your soul. Neither do our responsibilities for that matter. We can honor these people and afflictions where necessary without becoming shackled to them.

Freedom is our birthright — it's a state of mind.

Your thoughts and assumptions make the world as you know it to be true. Choose them wisely, or others will choose for you.

That is when you lose — when you sacrifice your happiness for others and end up without the dream.

As a fifteen-year-old, I had spent months attending school in a private hell. It doesn't sound a like a big crisis, but it looked very different back then. School and friends are a teenager's life. I was stripped of friendship, loyalty and bonding. I had cried myself to sleep each and every night.

The evening following the fight with Kylie my phone rang. It was her — the one who had turned my life black. I answered to hear her sobbing uncontrollably.

"What's wrong?"

"I'm calling to say sorry — I'm so sorry, Kim."

Long pause, then:

"It's okay."

It takes strength and character to say sorry. It takes a whole lot of heart and empathy to forgive. I may not be a fighter in the physical sense, but when the love is real and reciprocated authentically, I'll fight for love every time.

To this day, that friend remains one of the only two school friends I have kept in touch with, and she was worth the pain.

LOVE ON TIME

*K*im: Let's talk love. What does love mean to you, Mr X.?

Xavier: Dear Lord, I'm either a really good person to ask about love or really bad.

I guess I'm really good to ask because the synapses of my hopelessly romantic mind are always charged; sometimes overloaded with the electricity of love.

I'm not necessarily talking about the romantic comedy, neat little *"Sleepless in Seattle"* sweet tales of blissful moments where all the Instagram socialites hope to traverse the Empire State Building and find their soulmate.

Kim: Huh?

Xavier: I've been to the top of the Empire State Building and it was crowded and hot, and the lines rivaled Lightning Loops at Six Flags Great Adventure.

Kim: Hmm … I've been to the top of the Empire State building too. Yes, it was hot. It was August, 2007. Maybe you were there too. I'm sure that I spotted you among the billion other people crowding around.

Xavier: I was doing push ups as part of a push up challenge.

Kim: That's right, I remember now. You were the guy with the thingy...

Xavier: That's what she said.... lol

Kim: Heh. Good one.

Back to love …

Xavier: When my mind dives into the ocean of love, I see the happiness. But I also see the needed sacrifices along the way; the necessary crash course in understanding; the empathy, kindness and strength to not cut and run when the going gets tough.

Actually, it's a small miracle that I have it within me to still love with the strength of a tsunami after two divorces.

You would think I'd see love as an enemy.

Yet, it is the energy within my veins - the force behind every squeeze of my heart; the inspiration and sheer will of my consciousness.

Some people tend to refer to their "love life" when they really mean sex life.

I flip it around and try to live a life of love.

You see, in life, we are allotted a certain amount of time.

Kim: Hold on tight, folks, he's starting the number game! (he's a numbers guy)

Xavier: *clears throat and continues*

Let's assume you live for 100 years.

It is simple math - 365 days plus one leap year for every 4 years and 24 hours in a day.

Let's say in 100 years you have 36525 days or 876600 hours. That's not even a million hours of total time to live.

Subtract 8 hours a day for sleep (3 if you are me) or 289200 hours.

578400 hours left.

What percentage of your day is school, work, commuting, eating, mindless necessities of life?

Let's say 12 hours a day - 438300 hours of that (shit).

We are left with 140,100 hours.

Love doesn't just look at what it can do in the 140,100 hours of free time left. **It looks to maximize the 876600 hours and divides it by minutes and seconds and fractions of seconds to create the infinite within the given expanse of our time and space.**

Does that answer the question about love?

No. I'll keep going, but this is why I'm a bad person to ask about love. I can keep going and going like the energizer bunny, but my batteries are charged with an energy more electric than lightning.

Kim: And there you have it: Love on time divided by

minutes and seconds and fractions of seconds to create …
erm … just go love, people.

AWAKENING THE HEART CAN DO ANYTHING

But it takes a whole lot of courage to get there.

a rustic wooden heart dangles on a solitary, wrought iron candelabra that my son crafted during a metal workshop lesson some years ago. It's rough and wore-torn, and it leans slightly to one side but I love it. It stands atop a chest of file-drawers beneath the window in my office; a keepsake from his early teenage years.

I used to live in the Blue Mountains — a rugged stretch of dramatic ranges west of Sydney. It's one of those places that seeps into your bones and forever ensnares a part of your soul. Much like the moments before dawn when the sun emerges from the sea to leave you standing in a place of awe.

Nature has a way of stripping you bare when you

allow its essence to bleed into you. Connecting and grounding to our natural world is important in maintaining inner-balance and peace. They are some of the most precious moments existing throughout our lifetimes; created to nourish your soul and remind us of our humanity, as well as the eternal spirit within.

Have you ever gazed at the stars and completely surrendered yourself to their cryptic twinkles, or stood at a cliff top and succumbed to the glorious scene spreading before you?

It's deeply humbling and empowering at the same time.

You can literally feel yourself merge with the earth's spirit which sparks an undeniable connection to something far greater than yourself. It is through contemplating your bond with the universal spirit that will unlock the path to self-awareness and higher states of love.

God frolics among the forest treetops, snow-capped mountains and rugged coastlines. God waits for you to recognize yourself in each moment gifted to you, and every glance you didn't really see.

I'm not religious. At all. I don't adhere to any religious deity, and I do not use the word God in the context as such. To me, God is not a supernatural force who judges our earthly indiscretions, but term to describe source energy — the higher intelligence governing creation and all that is. The source of unconditional love.

Let's leave the judgement for the lower vibrations in our world. Those who are tethered to a set of rules and systems bred from fear and designed to control the masses. Unfortunately, it's difficult to escape the reality concocted by fear.

Blinders.

We are born shrouded by invisible blinders that conceal the truth of the divine resources available to us. Limitation is everywhere and shown to us at the onset. It's no wonder that we become so confused and frazzled as we move through life; that our mental health suffers beneath layers of pressure, stress and delusion.

Delusion for inauthenticity, and for the perceived limitations that we allow to determine the choices made from a closed mindset. Choices made from fear — the opposite of the unconditional love we should be aspiring toward.

Often, it is our most hearts desires that are left on the altar of authenticity. We learn to sacrifice deep love or passion because we believe that to follow our truths is too hard, selfish, or unattainable. We think we're not good enough, smart enough or talented enough.

We believe in those blinders.

The best hippie store ever is in those mountains west of Sydney. The owner travels the world to scour exotic foreign markets in India, South East Asia and South America to gather the most exquisite, rare and usual pieces and trinkets for his store. Which actually resembles some place you might find in an obscure market alleyway in Turkey. At least, that's what I envision.

The store was one of my most favorite places to visit when I lived in the mountains. That's where I picked up that old timber heart piece over a decade ago. The bold message etched across its face spoke to me:

Love. The heart can do anything.

It may sound a bit mushy for those who dismiss romantic notions, but opening the heart isn't just about romantic love. It is about choosing to live from your heart energy through practicing opening, clearing, cleansing, supporting and strengthening the heart space.

Consider this quote from Rumi:

"A thousand half-loves must be forsaken to take one whole heart home."

One whole heart home. Some of us are ready to forsake half-loves to take one whole heart home, but what does that mean?

It means courage.

Often, we forget to just sit with the feeling of love and allow its intense hues to fill us up until it overflows from our being. Life throws us so many challenges. We all tend to have a knack for switching off our hearts when it is convenient or when it seems too hard. The blinders close in all around us until we think there isn't enough love inside of us to go around or turn the impossible, possible.

Closing your heart means stagnation.

It means rejecting your life-force energy, which will serve to wither your soul and narrow the scope of your world. It means settling for discontentment, getting used to feeling unfulfilled and being afraid because it is through our hearts that connects us with others and allows us to feel compassion, empathy, **courage** and love.

Moreover, it is through our hearts that opens the channel toward realizing our connection to our sacredness — the key to transformation, joy and happiness.

Courage is vital to realizing out most fulfilling life.

It is true that the greatest forms of love we may encounter will be our most difficult to perceive and express — the precious whole hearted love you want to take home and keep forever.

These forms of rare love arrive to push us into greater states of awareness as they test our inner-strength and faith as our hearts reopen to love to a greater degree.

This is how the heart transforms us — through daring us to accept deeper spheres of love and contemplate new ways of thinking and being. A higher love that propels us into deep reflection, causing a significant a shift within.

It is the cycle of rebirthing your spirit.

The courageous heart is driven toward questioning the blinders to ponder higher-level concepts that will shatter preconceived notions and expectations surrounding love and limitation.

It is through a brave heart that will move you toward

fulfilling your passions, emerging into your truths and facing the challenges as you go deeper and quest longer in the name of love, self and expansion.

Transformation is a choice.

It starts with you. Allow the energy and wisdom of your heart guide you toward transformation and living a self-focused life paved with moments of creating greater awareness.

It is through love that you will expand your mind to see past the blinders and create new realities in the world. It is through contemplating your connection to the earth and universal spirit that will act as a springboard toward awakening your heart and accepting great love in your life; and ultimately each heart transformation affects us all.

It is time to trust in yourself that you may feel love, have compassion and find the courage to embrace all of life's sweetest offerings.

It is time to awaken your heart.

IS IT REAL? YOU MAY NEVER KNOW
UNLESS YOU WALK AWAY

Sometimes, you have to let it go.

*W*hen I first met my husband, we both had ex-partners floating around the sidelines of our lives. Having people on the sidelines is like moonlighting — they appear in your life as distractions, or as leisurely pursuits with mutual understanding that the relationship is on the fly.

That's not to undervalue those people in any way. Everything for a purpose, right?

My husband had enough moonlighting going on to fill a sin bin, so I can't be overly confident that his sideliners fulfilled anything meaningful, other than sex.

I couldn't escape them. We managed to bump into some of these women each time we ventured into town on a date. I was okay with it for the most part, unless the woman in question shamelessly flaunted herself all over him — which surprisingly occurred a lot. For some reason, the fact that he was no longer on the playing field was an unfathomable notion.

Hmm ...

The gift of indifference works well in those situations. I had it nailed. So much so, that when one ex-sideline floozy unabashedly approached him to resurrect an old game they'd often play, I met her victorious stare with a wink.

Her frazzled expression was priceless.

We all have a past. Those women were a dime a dozen. I can't really say that I was sound in the knowledge of his feelings for me at the time, because it was still early days.

But I *was* confident in me — in my worth as a person and as a woman, and what I have offer to the people in my life who love and respect me.

Everything. *Glory, glory!*

I loved him. Yet at the same time I knew that if he wasn't able to see the value in me, then it would be his loss and not mine. There is no mistaking it when it's real. You can't replace the deep connection that happens through the unexpected moments that leave you breathless, and the meaningful conversations that inevitably lead to hours of love making. More glory.

Exploration and fusion in every way.

I wasn't imagining it. He was there, connecting with

me. Intricate experiences of that nature with another person cannot be felt by just one party. It has to be reciprocated in order to reach a level of deep resonation. I knew it was more than a fly-by-sideline fling, even if he didn't admit it at the time.

Something magical happens when you meet someone special. You've got to believe in it.

There was one particular woman from his past drifting around who did manage to sneak under my cloak of indifference. *Mariska.* The one who he had loved before me. Everything changes when big "L" word is involved.

She felt like a threat even though she didn't live in the same country. She was some twenty-plus hour flight away and back in his hometown near Holland, and she was hellbent on rekindling their relationship.

It didn't help that he had her image propped up on his bedside table-cum-bookshelf in his tidy little bachelor pad, either. Photos taken from the instances when she'd flown out to visit him. Sparkling green eyes. Long golden hair … vivid grin.

Classic Dutch-clutch. Whatever that looks like.

She found out he preferred brunettes. Next thing, his email lit up with incoming updates; Dutch-clutch turned black.

Ah, Mariska!

Her name sounds like it should be in a Skid Row song. *I Remember You.* She remembered alright and she wouldn't let him go. Judging by the photos on his shelf, he wasn't letting it go so easily, either. Obviously, there was still something between them.

You know those early months in a relationship when you're still finding your ground and trying to figure out what the hell is actually going on? It was a bit like that. I could handle the sideliners, but I couldn't compete with love and I wasn't about to try.

So, I walked away.

I didn't kick up a stink; didn't accuse him of foul play or demand that he stopped corresponding with Dutch-clutch. I simply told him that I couldn't do it anymore and that I wasn't going to play second to anyone. **Period.**

I meant that shit. The thing is, you can never change the way people feel. It doesn't matter how much or how deep you love someone; they will always do what they're going to do regardless. And if the person you love doesn't love you back to the same degree, it is never going to be balanced enough to completely fulfil you, anyway.

Happiness in a relationship cannot thrive with doubt, suspicion, disrespect or distrust. This is where we trip up so readily when it comes to relationships. When we tend to accept less than what we know we deserve because we are in love — all of the opposite characteristics that deny a healthy relationship. Things like: Trust. Respect. Honor. Compromise. Dedication and great communication.

It is never easy to walk away from someone you love. I was already in deep and the pain was intense. Suddenly, every lyric to every love song killed. Lost love lingers like subtle poison. Yet sometimes, the act of letting go of someone is necessary and, believe it or not, it is the ultimate act of love. For the both of you.

There is truth to that old saying that goes something like:

"When you love someone let them go ..."

In the past, I've been forced to cut ties with people that I have shared time with and loved very much. Friendships that turned toxic and demanding. A family member who is not unlike the little girl with the curl in the middle of her forehead: *"When she good she was very, very good, but when she was bad, she was horrid."*

It's never an easy decision to discard those from your life who hurt you, but it comes down to self-preservation and protecting your quality of life. You can love someone safely from a distance. I've learned this and to this day, I still practice it.

Yet, when it comes to romantic love it can be excruciatingly more difficult to let go.

It didn't matter how many times I told myself that he wasn't right for me; that he didn't love me; that it was the wrong timing and it could never work out; I couldn't quite quell the yearning inside for him.

My heart fought my brain at every moment spent convincing myself that it was never real.

But sometimes, we have to walk away from love in order to discover its authenticity. Sometimes, it's the only way to know for sure.

About a month later, he called. Told me that he met me in his dreams and that he didn't want a life without me in it. It would be first time he uttered the words I had longed to hear.

I love you.

It took me walking away for the penny to finally drop. He returned a different man ready for the breadth of my love and all I had to offer — minus the Dutch-clutch and the sideliners, of course.

"… and if they return, they were always yours."

The truth is: When the right people come into your life, it can never be wrong timing. The right people are *timeless*.

THE UGLY SIDE TO ONLINE DATING

*S*ome time ago, my friend went through a period of using internet dating sites in search of romance. She was addicted to scouring the profiles of potential mates, selecting only the most promising prospects based solely on their pictures.

That's the thing about online dating sites, it's usually so far removed from authenticity that people are judged by a mere glance of a scrolling finger-you're lucky if you get a 3-second linger.

Online dating is a bit like choosing a prime cut among the crud in an inner-city meat market but worse, at least you know upfront what you're getting in a meat market.

Crud and all.

This was back when the online dating scene was in its early days and had just taken off like flying fish aplenty. My friend was hooked. It was during a time when we were both transitioning from our respective marriages and learning a new life as single mothers.

We spent a lot of time together back then. We took turns every other week cooking dinner for our combined children; we had movie nights and pizza nights on the weekends, and enjoyed quiet discussions over coffee while the kids were at school.

Every now and then, we would score a night away from our children to break out the heels and lipstick before hitting an unsuspecting dance floor in some dark hazy bar.

That was fun. I can't say that she wasn't my partner in crime at the time. She was bubbly, interesting and extremely cool to hang out with.

We all have that one outgoing friend who exudes bold confidence to the point it can get a little too much. This woman was so vain that she was almost a mirror. I don't mean it that in a nasty way. It's just the truth.

Honestly, she was and still is a beautiful woman. Bella donna. She is the perfect blend of Australian and Italian genes-buxom curves and full pouty lips; a flawless porcelain-like complexion that contrasted against a tumble of dark hair and equally alluring eyes.

She was a stunning sex-kitten who had me nicknamed Pussycat.

I won't tell you why.

When it came to our personalities, we were polar opposites. Her extroverted tendencies combined with her beauty attracted a lot of male attention and she thrived on it. Whereas, my introverted nature was much more reserved around new people.

My other friends at the time disliked her immensely. This was due to the fact that she was an outrageous flirt. No man was safe in her company. It made no difference if he was married and his wife was present-her full milky breasts would accidentally-on-purpose spill from her dress and her long lashes would batter like crazy in her attempts to ensnare his attention.

Most of the time, she succeeded.

She may have been somewhat shameless but it never really bothered me. I knew that beneath all of her outwardly improper behavior was a kind and generous heart who battled insecurity and self-doubt.

Sometimes, it is those who seek to find their self-worth through others who are the most frightened of life ... or the loneliest.

At the time, I was aware that these were the feelings driving her desire to find a romantic connection. It was through the opposite sex that she sought meaning and self-validation-and the way she internalized her own self-worth was the point her of vibration in attracting the men in her life.

Men who mostly treated her like used goods.

What I saw in her is what others could not or were unwilling to see and she loved me for that. It's funny how people are so quick to judge and label us. Yet, no matter how deep our conversations about life plunged, we couldn't land on the same page when it came to men and dating.

My approach to men and relationships was, well … rather incognito. Undercurrent. I wasn't interested in "catching" a man on Plenty of Fish, nor was I interested in dating. The thought made my stomach cringe at that time.

The way I viewed dating, love and relationships is the same way I look at everything in my life - if it's meant to be then it will be. Sometimes, the more we try to force something to happen in our lives, the further away it becomes.

I'm not always perfect at this; particularly when truths resonate deep in my heart with authentic connections, but I think that is part of the greatest lessons we come to learn throughout our lifetimes - to know when we have to release control over a situation.

This is who I am.

My friend and I had found each other in the early years after divorce when we were experiencing similar circumstances. The difference between us was that I chose to use those years alone as a time of deep reflection; hours spent whispering to the stars, reading spiritual books and discovering me; a time of unraveling myself from the inside out and introspection.

I knew that if I was going to allow anyone to claim a

piece of my heart again, it couldn't be anything less than the real thing.

Real love is a wild and tameless gift that will arrive to rattle your life when you least expect it. We hear that saying all the time, but it is true. You can never predict the appearance of the special ones, and almost always, challenges will accompany deep love because it is the only way that love can make a meaningful imprint on world.

When love carries enough strength and courage to overcome seemingly immovable obstacles, that's when the real magic of love prevails - when it shines bright enough to transcend and transform more than the actual partnership; when love changes the world.

That's the whole meaning of the power of love in a nutshell.

My friend wasn't thinking the same way about love. Her mindset lingered somewhere near desperation. She created profiles on various online dating sites and arranged frequent dates with men - all of whom turned out to be jerks.

Then she'd complain that the men she was meeting from online were shallow and were only after sex. Don't get me wrong, I mentioned that she was no angel. She enjoyed the game just as much as the fellows, and she was a royal prick-tease. But no sooner would she sleep with them, then there would be a man-sized hole in her bedroom wall with a blazing flame leading away from her.

Her quest to find love and be loved became a continuous cycle of failed attempts at connection that inevitably resulted in tears and heartache.

Until she met Nathan-another result of an online dating forum.

Nathan was a thirty-something good-looking guy with a positive outlook and a gentle demeanour. He was also a widower, having lost his wife and six-month old daughter in a tragic car accident the previous year.

He wooed my friend like a candlelit dinner and it wasn't long before she ditched the games to open her heart to new love. She was smitten. He was everything she ever wanted-he was considerate and attentive to her needs, he was kind and lavished her with affection, and the sex blew her mind.

Pièce de résistance.

She was a different woman who got the whole cake to eat. They began making plans for the future-Nathan wanted to move in with her and her children. He spoke about traveling together and they even talked about marriage.

The months rolled by and my friend began to notice that sometimes Nathan would perform a vanishing act. Days would pass without so much of a word to her text messages and phone calls. She put it down to the demands of his job and she knew that he still had moments where he struggled to come to terms with the death of his wife and baby.

Then, one day my friend received a phone call that would rock her foundations.

It was Nathan's wife.

Turned out, she and the baby were still very much alive and she was still very much married to Nathan. Somehow, Nathan's wife had discovered my friend's role in her husband's life and worse still, she wasn't the only one. Nathan had a long list of women on the side who he had met online and had believed his widower story.

My friend was broken and I broke for her. Nathan took cheating to a whole new level when he branded his wife and kid dead. That was the part I found the hardest to fathom - that someone could go there.

Was this an episode of Bold and the Beautiful?

I'd often jokingly compare her life with that analogy, but it didn't feel like a joke anymore. It felt devastating. Especially during the following months spent listening to her talk it through and cry for the heart she gave away to someone undeserving.

After the initial shock wore off, she contacted Nathan to ask him why he did it - she needed clarity about his reasons for telling her that his wife and child had died because that story was such a radical lie, that she had to find a way to process the experience.

His answer was as deplorable as the act itself when he said:

"Because it was a way to get you emotionally involved. When a woman has emotions for a man, the sex is a thousand times better."

It came down to sex. Just sex.

The experience with Nathan turned out to be the pivotal point in my friend's life. She didn't go back to her usual online hunting grounds, and she no longer concerned herself with the thought of finding a romantic partner.

Instead, she began focusing more on herself as a person; feeding her creative talents and taking night classes in accounting. She started to appreciate who she was on the inside and nourished that person enough to lift her self-depreciating thoughts to something more manageable.

Something that felt better.

She realized that love and respect cannot be found from a place of imbalance, and that we must first honor and love ourselves enough to receive the beauty of authentic love connections.

She had been looking in the wrong places for love the entire time.

What she discovered in herself was the courage to embrace a part of herself that she had kept long buried out of fear of being shamed and ridiculed.

She gave birth to her true nature of lesbianism.

These days, my lovely friend has found her love-bliss in the form of a woman who she is soon to marry. The two women have had to face many challenges in order to be together-from family outrage and protests, to finding a way to make it work what with her partner living overseas.

But in each other, they found the missing pieces and have managed to overcome the obstacles posed to them through their sheer dedication for one another-and no, they didn't hook up online.

The best thing about is that my friend is now experiencing a love that shines bright enough to impact the world because she and her partner were strong enough to rise above societal and family expectations to be together.

And that is the point of real and true love.

How can we not admire members of the LGBT community when the tribulations they face are some of the most challenging in the modern era?

The fact is that some of these people provide the greatest role models in today's society because they are among those who are breaking the invisible barriers and igniting change with love at the realm.

It is the bravest hearts on the path that will create new patterns of love in the world-if we stop looking in the wrong places.

14

LOST LOVE: WHY UNREQUITED LOVE IS INDISPENSABLE

"*I think you are the most wonderful person in the world.*"

Love and kindness are two of the greatest gifts we can give and receive in the world. I have been fortunate enough to receive love and kindness throughout my life. I've been even more blessed to have given my love freely. When expressed sincerely, love and kindness create a ripple effect in how we treat others. But sometimes, telling someone that you love them might produce the opposite effect.

It might see them running for the hills.

That happened to me once. I fell in love with someone who could never express his feelings in the same way. Granted, the circumstances were less than ideal, but that's the thing about love – it doesn't acknowledge rules. It creeps up and catches you unaware until one day you look up to see your heart cracked and bleeding over your sleeve as you wonder what the hell went wrong.

This love was different to any kind of love I had ever known.

This love showed me what it meant to love without expectations. The lessons were intense and at times, extremely tough. He took me to the highest love-sphere and dropped me with as much velocity.

He seeped into my soul and mirrored back at me parts of myself that I never knew existed – perfection and creativity, buried insecurities, feelings of worthlessness and inadequacy, and even hostility.

He made me feel like a woman.

As it turned out, when I finally found the courage to openly express my feelings to my beloved, they were promptly met with indifference which was followed by the Holy Grail of rejection – silence.

"I may never see you or cry with you or get drunk with you. But I love you. I hope that you escape this place. I hope that the world turns and that things get better, and that one-day people have roses again. I wish I could kiss you."

— Valerie (V for Vendetta novel)

Almost overnight, he vanished into a ghost and left me to question my sanity and every interaction that had unfolded between us. You know the part where you replay conversations over and over in your head?

Yeah.

I spent hours picking through the pieces and trying to puzzle them together into something that made sense. Something that might ease the emotional turmoil.

It was a fruitless exercise. I had fallen so deep that I couldn't deny the heartache – I had to feel and allow the agony to become a part of me in order to move through it.

Anyone who has experienced a broken heart knows how dark the aftermath can be. Every day is a shadow, with sleep the only respite from the pain.

When we fall in love it is natural to want to bond with the star of our dreams. It can be just as easy to become confused when your beloved is giving off an array of mixed messages in return.

I admire people who are truthful and upfront in all facets of life.

Word salads can fast become a brain-fry. Life can be difficult enough without the added stress of uncertainty when it comes to the people we love.

But it was uncertainty and word salads that became the prominent theme in this instance. My feelings were negated to the point that I had to assume it was unrequited love; even though I sensed and felt his deep affection and reciprocation.

Philosopher Friedrich Nietzsche on unrequited love:

"Indispensable to the lover is his unrequited love, which I would at no price relinquish for a state of indifference."

Unfortunately, my fellow didn't see things in quite the same way as Nietzsche. Which inevitable resulted with my heart feeling as if it was stuck between two continuously slamming truck carriages.

I was unbelievably screwed up.

They say that it's better to have loved and lost than to never have loved at all. That the damage caused by love lost and separation gives rise to growth and maturity, and the advantages are long-term when considering the bigger picture. Things like life-lessons, personal growth and expansion.

I guess it's true.

The experience did get me thinking about love and relationships from a different perspective. Even though it was difficult for me to understand how my love could be met with such carelessness, I wondered how it could have come to be.

Why are some of us willing to take a risk in getting vulnerable and expressing our feelings more than others?

Naturally, my focus immediately shifted on myself.

Rejection breeds feelings of shame, self-doubt and worthlessness, and I couldn't help but wonder what was wrong with me.

Was I not good enough for him? Not young enough? Attractive enough; talented enough? Was too outspoken and honest? *Does my personality totally suck?*

I could go on …

Eventually, I stopped the self-depreciating thoughts

and realized that it wasn't me who lacked the right qualities to attract love. What is right anyway? I am not inadequate as a person. I have a lot to offer the people in my life, and the world. I am perfectly imperfect, and for better or worse, I have learned to love who I am.

Someone has to; it may as well be me.

Sometimes, we have to choose to ignore the effect others have on our self-esteem and push past the insecurities long enough to recognize our own unique beauty and place in the world. There is only one of me.

There is only one of you, too.

Isn't it utterly superb that each of us brings our own flavor and essence into the world? Our experiences, the way we interact with one another and our environment is vastly different. This includes the way we love.

So, I dug in a little and discovered that when it comes to matters of the heart, the answer to how we love could actually lie in the past.

Let's explore.

When I was growing up, my parents showed me the value in expressing love openly. The words "I love you" were never withheld or negated. They were given and received each day of my life – even if I had misbehaved or displeased my parents in some way.

I was shown kindness, empathy and compassion, and I was secure in the knowledge that I was loved. These ways of being and expressing love have guided my parenting style and how I've raised and continue to raise my own children.

I realized that the open expression of love demonstrated to me by my parents as a child has also greatly influenced the way I love other adults as an adult. When I love, I am more likely to express my feelings freely because that was how I was raised.

That's my lovemap.

It is through our early relationships with our parents and caregivers that help us to create a "lovemap" that persists with us throughout our lives. Austrian neurologist Sigmund Freud called this "transference". He pointed out that when we find a love object we are actually "re-finding" it – a phenomenon that explains individuals who select a partner who reminds them of their mother or father.

Some of us have been there.

Personally, I love the concept of the lovemap because it gives us a foundation on which to identify the grand, often confusing and complex wildfire notion of love.

The lovemap concept was originated by sexologist John Money in his discussions of how people develop their sexual preferences. It captures the essence of a person's emotional and internal blueprint for their ideal erotic and sexual situations.

From Wikipedia:

"Money describes the formation of an individual's lovemap as similar to the acquisition of a native

language, in that it becomes established at an early age and bears the mark of the person's unique individuality, like an accent in a spoken language."

Once formed, the lovemap is extremely difficult to alter.

But it was Freud who really put sex on the map. He realized that human beings were sexual beings right from the start, positing the controversial theory that even babies have erotic feelings.

Considering the above concepts and conclusions offered by these brilliant minds, I think it's safe to say that the way we define ourselves as sexual beings and express love in our relationships essentially comes down to our upbringing.

The more attentive and loving our parents were, the more likely those qualities will shine through us.

Some of us have been shown the tools at the onset on how to deal with high-level emotions, express our love and get vulnerable with our feelings. Still, all the research and knowledge in the world doesn't take away an aching heart or the moments of incredible longing for your beloved.

Those are the moments when I tap into his essence and send him a burst of love. Love in silence is just as powerful as loud love. It doesn't matter that he cannot reciprocate my love because love doesn't require conditions in order to breathe and thrive.

I can honestly say that I am not the same woman

since him. It was his appearance in my life that showed me how to love to different beat, and I still consider him to be the most wonderful person in the world.

Nietzsche was right, unrequited love doesn't have to be lost love. It is indispensable.

15

4 THINGS WOMEN IN THEIR 40'S REALLY WANT IN A MAN

We're not demanding. We just want what we want.

ears ago, my girlfriends and I relished the quiet hours when we'd steal away from our male friends to sit beneath the stars with a drink and embark on deep and meaningful conversations.

Seems like a lifetime ago.

As eighteen-year-olds, we did this frequently. Girls need other girls. We need to talk and be heard, and there is nothing like a girlfriend's ear. We're good at it, too. It's like soul and heart therapy wrapped up in a special friendship bundle. Back then, it was boys and relationships that dominated the conversation, and sometimes, Michael Hutchence.

Star of my teenage dreams.

Mmm ... where was I?

I don't see my old friends too often nowadays. We are a far cry from those Michael Hutchence lovesick girls who shared everything and cried together over the most trivial things (okay, the bourbon may have played a part in that bit).

Life happens. Rock stars die too young and lone strands of rebellious hair appear in places it never did previously. But, every now and then, I am able to snatch a few wonderful hours with my friends to touch base and catch up.

Women need other women. We need to share deep secrets with someone who really understands us. Most of my emotional strength has come through the support of my sisters throughout my life. We give each other an outlet when most needed.

The conversations may have changed over the years, but the deep bonds have only strengthened. Unsurprisingly, men still seem to wind their way back into our discussions.

During a recent get-together, I recently asked them what a 40-something woman looks for in a man.

Ready to be a fly on the wall?

Here are the four most vital qualities that prevailed from the conversation:

(Disclaimer: the following is not professional advice and subjective material discussed by a few Aussie women who just know this stuff.)

1. **Please don't compare us to younger women.**

Compliments are wonderful. Some 40+ women might be in great shape and appear younger than their age – but we don't want to be compared to a woman in her 20's or 30's because, well, we're not her.

It is true that some men in their 40's and beyond want a young "trophy" on their arm. It's probably safe to say that every woman in her 40's has at some point contemplated if her significant other has toyed with the idea of trading her in for a younger version.

We've all seen The First Wives Club.

Thankfully, some men do prefer the love of a mature woman who knows how to handle her man. He recognizes that women of a similar age as him are the women he can relate to since they share a common demographic.

Women value a man who sees life the way we do; who sees us for who we are and what we have to offer – confidence. Among other things.

Time might have passed in a blink of an eye but we are in our 40's - we have self-knowledge and life experience, and we've earned every inch of those golden nuggets. We know who we are and what we want. In return, we would very much like those qualities to be appreciated by our men.

1. **Mature women do want romance.**

Just skip the flowers. Did anyone ever say this out loud?

We might be outliers on this one, but check it out:

Giving a woman flowers is a lovely gesture. They smell nice and they're pretty, but we have enough to do without hunting down an elusive vase, trimming stems and combining a sachet of sugary life-prolonging powder into water before arranging the bouquet just so.

This is unduly followed by days of cleaning up the wilting petals and making sure the water doesn't dry up.

In short, we don't want anything that requires us to do extra work.

Quality romance to a woman in her 40's is attentiveness and time. We want to feel the connection. We want to be "wooed" through acts of consideration, respect and support, and we want to feel special.

Many of us are working long hours in our careers. It's much more romantic and meaningful when a man takes the time to learn how you like your tea rather than to receive flowers.

1. **No game-players.**

"I don't want to pretend to be anything I'm not, and quite frankly, I'm too tired to deal with someone pretending to be something they're not."

True story.

We've said it before and we'll say it again - don't

bring the games. We're too … erm … old and too tired for the ring-around. Time is precious. We don't want to waste it on games when what we want is someone special.

Women in their 40's have been through their fair share of relationships and marriages. We have learned from those relationships enough to be in tune about what we want from a man, and we're ready to get it right.

Mature women are looking for a genuine man who practices kindness and lives from the heart. Someone who will treasure her heart enough to never let her down.

What we want is an emotionally-sound and self-realized man who can express his feelings and take responsibility for his actions; one who knows the value in time, love and vulnerability.

In simple words, it is an authentic connection that mature women want.

1. Self-awareness is key.

It is a special man who can steal and keep the heart of a woman in her 40's. She yearns for soul-quality. Someone who understands himself. He is on the same page as her, has learned from past relationships and is not interested in repeating old behavior patterns.

Let's be honest, the prospect of great conversation with an intelligent man is extremely appealing to a woman in her 40's. In fact, it's a damned turn-on. There is a reason why the human brain is the most powerful sex organ – use it.

Narrow-mindedness, stinginess and nit-picking are a big no-no. Let the small things slide and learn to laugh at yourself.

Humor is sexy.

So is thoughtfulness.

We are women who appreciate a man who contemplates higher-level concepts and life meaning. Someone with a broad perspective and possesses the ability to focus on the bigger picture.

And while we're talking self-awareness, a little (or a lot) of that quality won't go astray in the bedroom either – an unselfish lover makes the world go-around … and around.

And around.

Life is really a journey toward self-actualization. We're in it together. Regardless of what life-stage we are at, wise is the man who recognizes the gift of a woman's heart - a gift that should be cherished.

Real love is a treasure-trove waiting to be discovered through true connection. At the end of the day, that is what women in their 40's desire in a partner. At least, these women.

I WAS A PORN STAR
UNTIL I WASN'T.

*H*e didn't like to watch porn when he was eating. It made his stomach curl. Other than that, porn was fair-game at any time of the day.

I'd often wonder just how many variations of Cowgirl Beats the Doggy or Double Penetration a person could handle watching before it became brain Piledriver.

Remember when Facebook used to be rife with quirky quizzes? Back when virtual-socializing began to skyrocket.

One time, he sent me a multiple-choice quiz that was titled "Name the Star".

I can do that, I thought.

I opened the quiz to find an array of strange faces. Apart from Pamela Anderson, the names and images were unfamiliar.

End of thought.

It was a quiz for porn stars. He got them all right. He was proud of himself, too. Until I expressed my disbelief. As I formed the words "porn-junkie", his smile turned into something awkward.

I mean, who watches porn and actually knows the names of all of the porn-stars?

A porn-fucking-junkie, that's who.

Have you ever wondered how having sex on camera actually constitutes a "star" status?

I don't think it takes a whole lot of talent to fuck on camera as much as perseverance. Honestly, the inner-grit it must take to smile and not cringe when a guy cums all over your face is commendable. Not to mention the ability to fake ecstasy while receiving a fist-fuck.

Ouch.

When we got to the bedroom his addiction to porn really hit home. He had me pinned as some kind of Kimmy Granger; and yes, I just Googled for that name and learned that she's one of the world's most energetic porn stars.

Go, Kimmy.

He had assumed that I was an atomic blast in cum-space who secretly longed to be slammed via anal and have my eyelashes dripping with cum.

Imagine his surprise when he realized that I was no Bull Job. I'm not into being Doubled Stuffed, my legs don't bend over my head and I sure as hell don't want cum in my eye.

That doesn't mean I'm not adverse to trying new things in the bedroom. Rather that my idea of a satisfying time in bed is much less about body slamming and being railed from above and more about sensuality and connection.

Porn is not sensuality.

For an industry worth somewhere in the billions and easily one of the most influential phenomenons in our culture today, porn sure as hell misses the mark when it comes to portraying women's sexual pleasure.

The perplexing part is that people the world over experience their first exposure to porn between the ages of 12 and 14, serving as their first exposure to sex. That's a whole of young people learning thwarted sex practices, as well an objectifying imagery of women.

People who are exposed to porn are more desensitized to sexual violence in real life, too. Like rape, pornography is designed to exploit and dehumanize women.

The study: *Effects of women's pornography use on bystander intervention in a sexual assault situation and rape myth acceptance*, states:

"Participants who recently watched porn were less likely than those who hadn't to, upon hearing a description of a rape, call it a rape"

Proving the significant detrimental impact on how men view women and how women view themselves. It seems to be growing worse.

In her article: *5 Truths About Porn That Often Get Overlooked,* Mary Rose Somarriba says:

"The reason why the pornographic imagery online continues to get more and more extreme in intensity is because after repeated exposure, the human brain needs more shocking content to reach the same physiological effect."

This is when the same content that used to create great arousal no longer cuts it. To reach that dopamine fix, the content needs to be intensified. It's neuroscience.

About 90 percent of imagery in porn portrays aggression against women. A disturbing revelation considering the fantasy of porn often illustrates this as pleasurable for women.

I experienced firsthand the effects porn had on one man's psyche. It was just as well that I was able to assert myself in the bedroom enough to express my disinterest at performing unthinkable sex acts. But this may not be the case for every woman when facing the distorted images porn imprints in their partner's minds.

Mary Rose Somarriba concluded:

"This cultural thinking that porn is harmless is just like the content itself—closer to fantasy than reality."

It may appear dire, but all is not lost; not every man is into watching porn. Some men actually reject it. While porn might provide an arousing voyeuristic experience in the lives of many, some men do realize that it lacks to

KIM PETERSEN

convey and teach the true meaning of sexuality - which is ultimately love.

Love is the desire for fusion.

"It is sexuality that provides us with a human outlet and a human expression of divine love."

U.S Andersen.

Porn cannot demonstrate or show us the way to manifesting our full sexual power.

True sexual power is the ability to claim and mindfully channel your beautiful erotic self and sexual energy. It is the sacred linkages to your body and spirit; to a lover and to the universe.

It's the ultimate blend of sexuality and spiritualty.

A key aspect of sexual power is emotional intimacy. The instinctive desire to bond to your lover and be known. This makes the difference between pure physical sex and lovemaking.

Now, that's the stuff made of dreams.

Reverse Cowgirl, Ball Gags and Bull Jobs might quench an insatiable addiction to porn, but watching people perform those acts cannot simulate the qualities of a good lover.

In real life and between each couple, there is an electric chemistry that is unique to them. Things like: Scent, voice, touch, and kissing style.

Beyond these, in her book *The Ecstasy of Surrender,* Judith Orloff MD characterizes the 10 qualities of what makes a good lover:

- You're a willing learner
- You're playful and passionate
- You make your partner feel sexy
- You're confident, not afraid to be vulnerable
- You're adventurous and willing to experiment
- You communicate your needs and listen to your partner
- You make time and don't rush
- You enjoy giving pleasure as much as you enjoy receiving it
- You're supportive, not judgmental
- You're fully present in the moment with good eye contact and can let go

Porn be damned.

I'd take playful and passionate and good eye contact, along with emotional intimacy over a Piledriver any time of the day. Even when I'm eating.

17

5 WAYS TO TELL A WOMAN THAT YOU LOVE HER WITHOUT SAYING I LOVE YOU

"Once a man wins a woman's love, the love is his forever. He can only lose the woman." — Robert Brault.

I love you. It doesn't always mean what we might think. Depending on who's saying it or in what context those words are spoken, they can mean everything or nothing.

Sometimes, we fling those words out casually.

Like a universal-style kind of love.

For instance, we "love" the postman when he delivers that long-awaited package, or experience affectionate feelings when our favorite barista nails the perfect brew each time we pick up a coffee to-go.

These people are not necessarily important to us in a personal sense. More on a broader scale kind of way.

Saying "I love you" can easily become a customary habit between couples, too.

My husband once told me that he hated saying those words out of habit, as was the case during his long-term relationship prior to meeting and marrying me. He said that he ended up saying them to his partner not because he felt it at the time, but because it had become routine in that relationship.

Others may experience the opposite and find it difficult to say those 3 little words in the first place. It is an act of vulnerability and let's face it; opening our hearts to someone we love can lead to potential pain, loss or rejection.

"Love is easy", said nobody — ever.

But when we genuinely care about another person, it is important to be able to express our feelings. This might sound like a cliché, but it is so true when they say that life is too short to procrastinate when it comes to the important stuff like love and connectedness.

Time passes us so very quickly. While we may not be able to avoid regret in its entirety, we do have the power to select the parts of our lives where we might be able to avert regretful feelings.

A woman needs to know and feel in her heart the love of her man.

Saying "I love you" to your woman and meaning it is critical. But if you're finding it difficult to form those words right now, showing her can be just as, if not more effective.

In fact, when the feelings run deep and intricate within, there may not be enough words to convey and justify the intensity of your feelings. Some forms of love are unbelievably powerful.

Love has a language all of its own.

In his book, *The Five Love Languages: How to express Heartfelt Commitment to Your Mate*, Gary Chapman says that "Each of us has a primary love language. The key is we have to learn to speak the language of the other person."

According to Chapman, there are five ways people express love:

- Words of affirmation
- Quality time
- Receiving gifts
- Acts of service
- Physical touch

The secret to learning another person's love language is all in the observation. We tend to naturally express and give love in the way we prefer to receive love.

This might sound much simpler in theory than in practice. Love is a complex phenomenon driven by the wings of emotion. It can easily become a perplexing puzzle to determine your partner's preferred love language — particularly between the sexes.

When your woman has a firm understanding of your love for her, you're more than half-way there to conquering the perplexing love-puzzle. But if you are struggling to form the words she longs to hear, she may be unsure of where she stands with you.

This is when misunderstandings can arise in a relationship.

Here are 5 sure-fire hacks to expressing your love without saying "I love you":

1. Listen to your woman

Affirming words don't always need to be the big "3".

Listening with an open heart and mind can speak volumes in expressing love for a woman.

Women need to be heard and understood by their men — not just to the words we are saying, but to the feelings we are trying to express. When a woman is heard by her man, she knows that he cares for her, and that her feelings are important to him.

Listening is a fundamental relationship promise — when we truly hear what another person says, we open the door to being seen as worthy of trust. Higher performing relationship right there.

2. Have her back

If words can cut deeper than a knife, then actions are salt on the wound.

One of the best things about being in a relationship is

knowing that you always have someone in your corner — and one of the biggest turn-offs for a woman is when the man she loves flakes out on her.

With the world full of billions of people, we need to know that there is a place just for us when it all becomes too much — for a woman, this sacred place is often within the comforting embrace and support of her man.

We need loyalty and courage to fuel the foundations of love, and we need a man who is willing to stand by us in the face of adversity, peer pressure and other challenges life presents.

Women don't want to guess if her man will be there for her. In the end, it's our support for each other that acts as the invisible glue bonding us together.

3. Be forgiving

The ultimate act of love is forgiveness, and there is no better way to love someone than to openly forgive and forget.

Look, we all screw up and nobody gets it right all of the time. Including your woman. She might be your Goddess, but she is far from perfect. She is your *special* woman — you must be willing to love her imperfections and nuances as much as the rest of her.

A woman appreciates a man who sees her for who she is and has the capacity and maturity to see beyond her indiscretions without passing judgement or ridicule.

Clinging on to resentment, pointing out failures and holding grudges is like pouring hot toxic liquid into your love. It's love with conditions and not real love at all. Nothing positive can be achieved by festering on the past.

Being able to fully forgive and move on means inner-freedom, too — it is an act of understanding, empathy and compassion that will actually set you free.

Whatever happened yesterday — bridge it and focus on the good stuff instead.

4. Admit to your mistakes

This one rolls with forgiveness; the blame game is a nasty game.

Let's not go there anymore.

A woman values a man who is open and honest with his imperfections; who can admit to the wrongs he may have caused and attempts to make amends without pointing fingers.

This shows her that you're willing to accept responsibility for your mistakes rather than to pass the buck onto others. It also shows her your strength and character, and promotes trust and security within the relationship.

It is your willingness to be vulnerable that will truly convey the depth of your feelings for your woman.

5. Touch her

The truth is in the touch.

A lover's touch is a powerful touch. She needs to feel you intimately, and she craves to touch you in return.

Once we get past the gropy, touch-for-the-purpose-for-acquiring-sex stage, physical touch is really about strengthening the existing emotional connection.

So many of our intimate feelings can flow from the act of touching. It plays a critical part in enhancing and developing love because through touch, we become vulnerable and open to our lovers. We want to connect and trust someone; and we need our lover's arms to escape from the world.

Physical touch is important in that it really confirms all of the other ways we express our love for our mates. Even the briefest touch from another person can elicit strong emotional experiences.

It will be in your touch that tells her how much you love her.

Ultimately, we are all creatures seeking meaning and love in the world through the connections and relationships we form with others. But taking the time to express your feelings to the woman you love will grant you access to a place you will never want to leave; Robert Brault was right when he said that a woman's love is forever.

It will be up to you to value and keep it.

18

WHAT DOES A GENTLEMAN LOOK LIKE TO YOU?

A gentleman, while antiquated as a term, is a description of one with grace. Isn't it odd that we call a civil man a gentleman and a woman who carries herself with self-respect, a lady?

- Xavier Eastenbrick.

*M*y mother used to tell me that I was a beacon for jerks.

She was right. Somehow, I had a knack for attracting men who play games. Dangerous games that hurt me. Men who thought it was okay to treat me as some kind of possession.

Question: Does a gentleman devalue a woman?

Answer: A gentleman never lies to a woman — he should go out of his way to never make her cry unless they are tears of happiness. He always treats her like a lady.

- The Gentleman's Journal.

Some men have an ingrained sense of entitlement. They think bedding a woman equates to ownership. I remember reading somewhere that this sense of "ownership" over a partner actually sticks with these men even after that particular relationship dissolves.

Take my ex-husband for example. Long after our divorce, he would still call me with all kinds of unreasonable demands and questions. More than once, I had to remind him that we were no longer married.

He didn't back off until I married someone else.

It comes down to emotional maturity.

If you Google the phrase, "when do men emotionally mature", you'll find the magic number is forty-three.

It's thirty-two for women. That's a whole lot of years for a woman to wait for the penny to drop. Even then, it isn't always a given.

I'm not convinced that all men in their forties are actually emotionally mature. Some women, too. I have encountered mature women who exercise emotionally manipulative tactics, and men who exhibit behavior like a five-year-old — as if they have chronic man-flu.

Constant complaining, gaming and knee-jerk reactions all round. Not so hot for developing strong bonds and trust with others.

Question: Should a gentleman do the Moonwalk?

Answer: No one wants to see a grown man Moonwalking and grabbing his testicles on the dance floor anymore. Let it go. Literally.

No one wants to see a grown man clad in a pair of skimpy Speedos at the beach, either. We refer to them as budgie-huggers here in Australia.

Sometimes, the "huggers" don't quite hold all of the budgies, if you know what I mean. Sometimes, less is actually *not* more.

A gentleman should be open-minded though.

An intelligent man knows the benefit of listening to other's views and being prepared to learn and develop his own world view. He seeks to broaden his perspective.

He doesn't judge, either.

Nor does he ever tell.

Uh-uh. A gentleman has no interest in Chinese whispers, vicious gossip or running others down. He doesn't shoot off at the mouth before thinking, and he doesn't always have to have the last say.

There is something to be said about thinking before responding — a small window of time exists where you get to choose how you respond to the situation confronting you.

Sometimes, it might be even longer. Make it count.

A gentleman learns to quell the knee-jerk reaction; he carries himself with dignity and respect at all times.

When my parents divorced, my mother ran into the arms of a much older man. Like, thirty years much older. At first, I tried to resent him. He wasn't my dad. That resolve didn't last, though.

Ron was a gentleman. Old school style.

Question: Do they even make them anymore?

Answer: In this day and age, grace is often sacrificed on the altar of selfishness, greed, and convenience.

- Xavier Eastenbrick.

Ron opened doors for my mother and showed her what it meant to be treated like a lady. *A lady* (check out featured image). I don't know that that skill is common these days.

Not really.

Question: Should a man open a door for a lady in this day and age?

Answer: This time-honoured gentlemanly gesture has become problematic in the modern world. For a lady, a gentleman always offers his seat, opens the door and helps her with her luggage.

- The Gentleman's Journal.

Hmm … interesting.

Which leads me to …

Question: Do men actually sacrifice their comfort for a woman?

Answer: Offering your coat to a lady is an act of attentiveness and selflessness. A gentleman should always offer his coat to a lady, walk her home and offer to pay.

- The Gentleman's Journal.

I asked my fifteen-year-old daughter what a gentleman looked like to her.

Answer: Respectful. Considerate and not selfish.

Good answer.

"Do you think the boys at school behave like gentlemen?"

Laughs.

"No way!"

When does it kick in? When emotional maturity takes hold at ... umm ... forty-three?

She could be waiting until she's a middle-aged woman before she experiences a true gentleman.

I hope not.

Question: What does it mean to be a gentleman today?

Answer: The most common perception for a gentleman is a man who ensures that he is chivalrous towards women. The term attaches itself to men who are courteous and treat women with respect. **Gentlemen are attentive to what a woman wants and needs, yet in the same regard they understand their own value and purpose.**

- Brian Cornwell.

Historically, a gentleman was a way to describe a man

of character. The term gentleman has changed over the years, nowadays it's used to describe the actions and behaviors of a man.

Perhaps they should introduce these behaviors within the education system to reinforce what I hope is being taught at home. Things such as teaching boys how to become men who are polite, calm, respectful and considerate — the cornerstone for defining what it means to be a gentleman.

Vital qualities are necessary for forming and nurturing healthy relationships.

Question: What does the modern-day gentleman look like to you?

Answer: Here's what my views are about the quality that makes both a distinction above the base animal within:

It is the quality of grace.

We tend to have an image in our minds of a suit-clad man and a dress clad woman, but it isn't by any true measure the defining quality. Any brute can put on a suit and be as disgraceful as one clad in filth.

One with grace is polite as their default position, slow to anger and respectful of others.

One with grace is not fearful to stand up for what is right and express themselves with the truth of their intention.

One with grace doesn't manipulate to move ahead.

One with grace understands that they don't know it all and strives to be more than who they are.

A gentleman is caring and kind, strong and confident in that which matters.

- Xavier Eastenbrick.

Spoken like a true gentleman.

19

SEX AFTER DIVORCE CAN TRANSFORM YOU

Leave Your Inhibitions at the Bedroom Door

I was thirteen when I met my first husband, twenty-three when I married him and thirty-three when I left him. Strange. There seems to be an overarching emphasis on the number three at play here which I hadn't realized until this very moment.

Honestly, I'm not surprised. There is something magical about the number three. It is a sacred and significant number in many religions. There is a Trinity for Christians, Triple Goddess for the ancients, and the Celts believed that everything happens in threes.

Did you know that no other number holds more esoteric significance and power than the number "33"?

This is because thirty-three symbolises change and growth.

Coincidence? I think not.

Speaking of numbers, how does "69" resonate with you?

My mother turned sixty-nine last year. She came to my house so that I could cook her something special. I can't remember what culinary delights I dished up now, but I do recall repeating her newly acquired "magic" number throughout the evening.

It came out in random bursts and went something like this:

"Sixty-nine, mum. You can only say that you're sixty-nine for one year of your life-you better enjoy that ride."

Of course, my insinuating comments went over her head until my husband overheard and cracked up laughing. It was nearing the end of the night by then. She had blushed.

"Oh … is that what you meant?" [Insert fake shocked expression] "You are disgusting, Kim."

Heh. Takes one to know one.

Truthfully though, the number sixty-nine denotes balance, warmth and love on the spiritual level. Yin-Yang, idealism and equality. Like a glimmer in the eye. Light. Love. Flames, and the cycle of life.

However, 69 is slang for the much more commonly known practice of simultaneous fellatio-when two partners arrange their bodies to perform oral sex on one another at the same time.

My ex-husband was partial to the above-mentioned

sexual activity. I can't say that he wasn't skilled in that department because … well, he could eat. My God, he could eat.

Delightfully so.

It wore off rather fast though, because no amount of skilled tongue could make up for the endless hours spent enduring his demeaning verbal, emotional and physical abuse.

That's why I left him. After years of aching for change, I finally found the courage to make it happen at 33.

During the last years of my marriage, I rarely slept with my husband. By the time that final year rolled around the sex had diminished from almost nil to zero.

No more super-tongue. When the bad stuff outweighs the good stuff, you got to let some things slide.

Grin.

His tongue was still put to good use though-in the form of the protests and whines that inevitably followed.

It didn't matter how many times I had tried to talk to him about his horrible treatment, the reality of the situation wasn't quite gelling with the warped notions in his head-he didn't understand why my interest to be close to him reduced to nothing.

Moreover, he couldn't or wasn't capable of making the connection.

It's not rocket science. If you want your woman to

keep fucking you then don't treat her like garbage. Simple.

How is it that some men think they get to degrade and belittle a woman at every turn and then expect her to cop it sweetly and open her legs as if everything is fine and dandy?

Newsflash: It doesn't work that way. Bogan. That's what I have to say about that scenario. Do you know what he had to say about it in return?

"If you don't have sex with me, I'll be forced to find it elsewhere."

When a man says those words to me and my response is to shrug and throw out a "whatever" over my receding shoulder, things aren't looking so good for that relationship in the immediate future.

He eventually followed through in the form of a woman who lived interstate. God knows where he met her, but she took the pressure off me and for that I was grateful.

If I'm being honest, there was a part of me that felt compelled to warn her about his abusive ways. He was a brute.

As it was, I kept my mouth shut. Maybe I was being selfish for keeping his demons under wraps in those early years, but her behavior toward me was nothing short of hostile. She saw me as a threat. Of course, she couldn't have been further from the truth.

I would have given her my written agreement had she asked for it:

I, Kim Petersen, hereby grant you all territorial rights to my husband; including a lifetime of unlimited access to his super-tongue.

Good luck and God bless.

Almost another year would pass before I eventually slept with another man and had tongue-access fully restored again. If you are doing the math, you'd be correct if you worked out that I was dry in the sex arena for about two years solid.

Luckily, I owned a good vibrator (Okay, I owned more than one good vibrator).

We both hit the jackpot when he arrived on the scene. I ditched my vibrators for a man who was seven years younger than me and keener than a jar of hot English mustard. By that time, I was so ready to feel someone up close, that he didn't know what had hit him.

Sexual energy on steroids.

Exploration was the name of the game. I had reached a time in my life where the desire and need to know more about everything and anything was overwhelmingly strong.

Most of all, I needed to know myself.

So, I left my inhibitions and self-conscious feelings at the door of yesterday to embrace a new version of myself-a woman who wasn't afraid of change or expressing her desires to experience secret sexual fantasies; someone who was slowly beginning to like herself again.

I was on threshold of blossoming into a stronger and more self-assured person, and sex with a new partner played a vital role in that transformation because it somehow acted as a bridge from one reality of existence to another.

You could even say it was a sexual revolution.

It was through intimacy and connecting with a man who respected me that unleashed my inner Goddess and catapulted me into self-empowerment.

Something happens when you undergo a major life-change. It is as if a switch turns in your soul when you make a deliberate choice to take the road less travelled- when you decide to take a leap of faith, tackle the obstacles in your way and trust in something higher than yourself.

That's what I had done when I chose to leave my abusive ex-husband.

I left a man who had spent years running me down and trying everything in his power to break my spirit. And I did so with three children and an extremely grim bank balance.

Thirty-three turned out to be the pinnacle of new beginnings for me. An age that saw me embarking on a new journey paved with high and low moments-from despair and deflation, to appreciation and happiness.

I'd finally discovered the path to self-growth, expansion and the way to feeling inner-peace.

I'd finally found me-with the added bonus that the new man in my life turned out to be an extremely ardent student in the tongue department. God, could he eat ...

20

EMOTIONAL ENTANGLEMENT: DO YOU PHUNK WITH HEARTS?

inding someone who genuinely cares about you in today's world can feel like pushing shit up hill. Often, it can be difficult to see past yourself long enough to realize that not everyone you encounter is authentic in their intentions.

What I mean is that when you are genuine in heart, you tend to assume the same for others because this is the place from where you anchor your outlook on life. I hate to be the one to say it, but not everyone gives a flying phunk about your heart.

In fact, some people like to Phunk With Your Heart.

The Black Eyed Peas had it pegged when they crooned about it-a woman who wants to protect her heart while her fella runs a rapping dialog to convince her of his sincerity.

That guy claimed "crazy in love", but let's get real-life and relationships are not Hip-Hop love songs and we all don't glam it like Fergie.

Relationships are a bit like Lego. We sift and sort through the pieces, select that special someone and steadily build the relationship together. Sometimes, we might lose a few pieces along the way and our fragile Lego-hearts may break. So, we pick up the pieces and start again.

Occasionally, we may encounter that guy who had Fergie so doubtful-someone who actually relishes playing with our Lego-hearts.

Heart-Lego.

"No, no, no, no, don't phunk with my heart."

As the name suggests, Heart-Lego is when someone builds up your feelings; layering one piece after another until they've had enough or become bored with the game. Then, they break down the creation and leave your heart in pieces.

As a child, every so often my mother would take my brother and I into the city to visit Lego city-a city within a city. It was awesome. We would sit at tables brimming with Lego and build all sorts of Lego wonderment. When it was time to leave, we'd smash our creations to pieces ready for the next child to pick up.

I never built a Lego-heart.

My mother always told me to never play games with

people's hearts. She said that feelings are not a playground and people's emotions are not a game.

The same night I met my husband, I met another man. They were polar opposites. Simon was soft spoken and gentle, yet possessed a strong masculine quality. He worked in the health care industry, drove a pimped-up hearse and wore chunky black boots, studded belts and an array of cool Gothic accessories.

He was utterly fascinating.

We spent hours engaging in late night conversations about anything and everything, and he showed me glimpses of "the other side"-a dark and seductive side of life that was new to me.

Simon was unique in every way. He was mature and kind, a little bit twisted and somewhat dark, and he was into me. It wasn't long before I found myself in the midst of a love-triangle.

I didn't see it coming right away. I wasn't sleeping with him. I was sleeping with my husband, and despite spending time with Simon, I was careful not encourage anything other than friendship.

"I want your mind too. Interestin's what I find you."

When a man is genuinely into you, he leaves the games for Lego-city. He won't phunk with your heart because he cares for your heart. He doesn't want to hurt you.

He began sending me quirky text messages bidding

me goodnight right before bedtime, and his interest in me as a person grew-my feelings, dreams, (weird) ways of thinking and buried insecurities-he wanted to know all about them. He wanted to know what made me tick.

Simon was aware that I was seeing another man romantically, but this didn't seem to faze him. Although, after a while he was unable to keep the side-sniping comments from our conversations. He disliked my husband and began to make that fact clear.

But it wasn't until the night that he kissed me that things really became awkward.

What am I doing?

That was the question floating in my mind at the time.

On one hand, I had this amazingly solid man who made no qualms about what he wanted-he wanted a "partner in crime" and had his sights set on me. On the other hand, was my unpredictable future husband who was shooting off mixed signals faster than a lollipop man on Pitt Street.

Simon was everything I could wish for in a partner, and yet, there was something missing. It was the fire-the passion. He didn't send my pulse racing with a glance or induce butterflies at the thought of our next encounter, and there were no exquisite sensations going on in my panties when he touched me.

"My love for you is not iffy. I always want you with me."

I wasn't in love with him.

It was then that I realized that I might be behaving like one of those people my mother had warned me about-the kind that build on the feelings of others only to knock them down. Heart-Lego.

Guilt happened, and I felt horrible for my part in giving him false hope. I didn't want it to get so far that I would leave him in pieces. So, I let him go gently.

There is no way around it-phunking around with people's emotions is just not cool. It cuts both ways. You have to be upfront-even when we fall into emotional situations that catch us off-guard.

You might not be aware that your name brings a smile to someone's lips, or that you're on their mind all the time. But when they find the courage to put their feelings on the line for you, the way you respond is critical in more ways than you can imagine-for them and for you.

Unfortunately, there will always be people out there who have no respect or regard for the feelings of others or how their actions cause deep pain-the Heart-Lego players. That is why you must not assume that everyone is as kind-at-heart and as genuine as yourself.

Here's another piece of advice from mother-dearest:

Never give your beautiful heart away to just anyone. It's too precious.

It might be an endless lesson, but the way we handle high-level emotional situations and our relationships shows the true nature of our own hearts-and the only Heart-Lego building that should be happening between two adults is like the house Ed Sheeran sings about in his song, Lego House when he says: "I'm gonna pick up the pieces."

Otherwise, avoid the heart-phunkers and don't build on Heart-Lego if your intention is to knock it down.

21

HOW SHE REALLY WANTS TO LOVE YOU

And why you might be screwing it up

Forget young love. It's sweet and looks like crushed cherry blossoms on a greeting card. Fresh off-the-bat-romance. Brimming with yet-to-mature emotions and still-developing … well, everything really.

*W*ho really knows what they're doing in the realm of love when they're 21?

I remember those stormy and confusing-AF days, and I am glad they are behind me.

I can't tell you how many times I had packed my bag, ready to head to off to god-knows-where during the early years of my first marriage. Granted, he was an extremely volatile human being who completely did my head in; but we were young and still learning about ourselves. Not to mention trying to figure out how to be in a "grown-up" relationship.

I'm older now. Like most women my age – i.e. in their 40's, I have experienced my fair share of stormy love and heartache. Those experiences have penetrated into my psyche and imprinted my soul to form the woman I am today. A woman who has learned about herself, survived turmoil and great pain to finally emerge into a state of self-awareness.

I've learned a lot from past relationships. I wouldn't trade any of those loves for the world.

Every woman in her 40's is hoping – no, *praying* that you, dear male, have evolved from your past loves, too.

It's insane how much back-ground knowledge, insight and wisdom we gain through our relationships. Those experiences really do enrich the inner-layers to form the adults we become.

A friend was recently telling me that for those couples who meet early in life and stay together are more likely to stagnate when it comes to relating to and understanding the opposite sex to some degree. More around behaviors and emotional intelligence.

Whether there's truth to that theory, is not for me to say. It is an interesting and quite possibly valid observation, though. I can see how personal-growth may suffer when slipping into states of complacency in long-term relationships that begin during early adulthood.

Not all relationships grow with us as we mature and move through life.

Our hearts actually develop and open to love more deeply through the exposure of different relationships as each union is unique and offers us diverse and vital life-lessons.

Think about this:

A woman in her 40's who has experienced diversity in relationships knows how she wants to love her man.

She knows how to handle him and she knows how she wants to make him feel; and she wants to do all of this minus the drama.

Honestly, when one of these women decides to give her heart to a man, it's like the Holy Crucible equivalent of love. That might sound like a bold statement. I'm standing by it one-hundred percent.

I've experienced significant past relationships; I've loved with my whole heart.

My heart is different now.

I have loved and lost; my heart has bloomed and blossomed. I've bled, cleansed; rebirthed. Most importantly, my heart has transformed into the ability to give and receive higher states of love.

It is women who have learned from the past who are ready for a connection that encompasses EVERY possible element existing in a relationship.

Intellectually. Emotionally. Psychologically. Sexually. *Soulfully.*

Entirety.

I'm talking one badass, soul-satisfying quality relationship.

A *quality* woman knows where she wants to focus her energy. She has reached a point in her life where ordinary relationships no longer cut it or satisfy her insatiable need to connect authentically. **She wants more.**

She wants something beautiful to live for; and she wants to love you like this:

- She wants to sink into your mind and dance with your soul.
- She wants to laugh and play with you; explore your thoughts; challenge your ideas and tease out your vulnerabilities.
- She wants to be your strength; your soft and safe place when you need her.
- She wants to learn and speak your secret love language.
- She wants to give you her heart and open herself wholly to you.
- She wants to feel you; make love until the fusion becomes complete in beautiful and meaningful ways.
- She wants know you - but she also realizes the necessity for breathing space for the both of you; she cherishes her alone time.
- But she loves to want to share time with you;

as your friend and companion as you explore
life together.

- She wants you; and she *will* make you the
center of her universe.

Does this sound ordinary? A little unrealistic,
perhaps?

It doesn't have to be.

There is a reason why men have written about a
woman's love throughout the ages. Stories. Poems.
Songs. Men who have tasted, worshipped and cursed the
love of a woman. Men who know its worth and cannot
resist it.

So, where does it all go wrong?

It could be one or more of these three relationship-
killer attributes:

1. She's not your mother.

Look, we've all heard about the man who wants to
curl up in a foetal position, lay his head in his lady's lap
while she soothingly strokes his hair and whispers in his
ear. Similar to the way she might comfort her child.

Erm … no. Just no.

This might be the equivalent of a woman swaddling a
strap-on and demanding you get on all fours so she can
release her pent-up masculine energy and feel all-
powerful.

See where I'm going here? You cringed, right?

We do understand a man's yearning to be nurtured. We won't withhold that from you entirely. But please get your shit together - we don't want to feel like your mother. At all.

Psychology Today: *"For many married men, the wife may start to become a mother figure. She may encourage less play (hanging out with friends, heavy drinking) and behave in a more grown-up fashion. Here is the male take on this sea change: "Before we got married, she had fun, too. She and I would go to a club together, she would drink and we would dance. Now she wants no part of it. This mothering behavior often becomes even more pronounced when children enter the relationship."*

The article goes on to say that "both men and women need to understand that these learned roles are negatively impacting their relationships."

Other behavior aspects that may be helping to screw up relationships between men and women are simple really: Selfishness. Complacency. Entitlement Syndrome =

1. **Emotional Immaturity.**

I'm not pointing fingers. I'm not saying that every woman actually wants or even has the capacity to love in the above-mentioned ways, either.

A woman can be just as obsolete as her counterpart when it comes to the realm of love and relationships.

What I am saying, is that if we want a quality, grown-up relationship that supersedes the "ordinary", then we must reject old behavior patterns and inject the quality ones to build something beautiful together.

Emotional maturity means managing your feelings:

- Door slamming.
- The silent treatment.
- Unthoughtful language.
- Blaming.
- Keeping score.
- Being unempathetic.
- Carelessness.
- Inflexibility and resentfulness.
- Fighting unfairly.

Are all signs of emotional immaturity and won't foster an authentic connection with a woman.

It's all about mindfulness and being self-aware.

Let's get real – a healthy relationship won't thrive, grow or strengthen under these contrary and negative behavioral patterns.

No matter who is doing the door slamming.

1. **Sex isn't your right.**

This may come as a shock to some men: She might be your woman, but her body is her own and her sex isn't your given right.

Most of us do not withhold sex as punishment or use sex as *some kind management device for inciting compliance with our desires*. Acting as if she is deliberately restricting you from her thighs will actually do very little to help the cause. This is when sex becomes a chore.

You don't want that. Trust me.

Want to hear the truth?

If she isn't giving out, it's probably because:

1. She's too damned tired. Most of us are working long hours and organizing a household. At the end of the day, sex is often the last thing on our minds.
2. Hormones. They play havoc on a woman. Total killjoy. Cut her some slack and practice empathy.
3. You may just be in the habit of behaving in some of the ways stated in the "emotional immaturity" section. No woman wants to make love to a man who still acts like a child or who thinks he is entitled. At least, not for long.

The truth is, women want their men to see them as

sexual beings just as much as men want their women to find them desirable. While sex is important in keeping the romantic flames burning and the connection real, the reality is that for many women, so many other factors come into play when it comes to the bedroom department.

At the end of the day, women don't need their men to prove how macho and manly they are. They don't need a man-child, either. They just need men who are willing to meet them halfway and who take the time to understand them, treat them fairly and equitably – and that is all is takes to transform an ordinary relationship into something much more fulfilling and meaningful.

Something beautiful to live for.

That's all it takes if you want to penetrate your woman fully. It will be in this moment that she will open herself to love you the way she really wants to love you; and that's a love worth striving for.

22

HOW I ATTRACTED THE RIGHT KIND
OF LOVE INTO MY LIFE

It's not as impossible as you might think.

*L*ike attracts like. The Law of Attraction states this as true. If you're emitting a low vibrational frequency, you will attract a mate with similar insecurities because these feelings are your underlying point of attraction. Flip it around to higher vibrational pulses, and you will find these qualities reflected back at you.

It's an energy thing.

This is why it is so important to do your inner-work. No one can do it for you. As we move through life, we're either going to realize the path toward inner-freedom and enlightenment, or we're not.

We're either going to realize the gift of a heart, get brave and be willing to reach for more in the realm of love, or we'll settle for something mildly pleasing for the sake of [fill in the blank here].

Men and women are wired differently. I get that. It takes dedication, patience, and a whole lot love to reach a mutually fulfilling relationship. When we are ready for something truly wonderful to come into our lives, all that dribble-nonsense and dissonance left over from past relationships must give way to insightful revelations.

In other words, if we're unable to learn from the past and adjust accordingly, then the chances of breaking new ground and opening the door for more satisfying and authentic connections are minimal.

Breaking these patterns can be tough.

There was a long period in my life when I attracted domineering and abusive partners. It began with my first boyfriend and continued with my first husband. It was when the marriage ended that I vowed to never allow a man to treat me so badly again.

And you know what happened?

The next man that came into my life was exactly like the others – Controlling. Selfish. Dominating. Tyrannical. A man who thought it was his God-given right to sweep into a woman's home, claim his throne and reign supreme over her and her children.

A man who assumed I would fall into line because I was a woman.

He displayed much of the typical characteristics of an abuser. The same attributes that I knew well. Things like:

- Excessive jealousy
- Extreme possessiveness
- Suspicion and paranoia
- Unjustified accusations
- Forced me to have sex when I didn't want to
- Spiteful and often vicious behavior
- Berated and belittled my way of doing things; my viewpoints and sense of self
- Desire to isolate me from my family and friends

I could go on.

I couldn't believe it. I remember wondering what was wrong with me to have attracted the same kind of man in my life. I wasn't any of those characteristics mentioned above. I wasn't an asshole. I wasn't mean or selfish. I'm still not any of those things.

So, why then, did the same kind of man and experiences keep showing up in my life?

Low self-esteem and feelings of self-worthlessness reveal themselves in a variety of ways for different people. For some, the need to dominate and control is the means toward a false sense of empowerment. For others, it is the buried feelings of inadequacy that uphold mistreatment in our lives.

It may not even be a conscious thought. Just a lingering bend deep in your psyche confirming that you deserve to be nullified by another human being; that you are not worth any more than what you're getting.

Those are the same feelings that abusive people play on. They know that by breaking you beyond repair will grant them more power to manipulate and control the relationship.

No more of that. Please, no more.

That's what I was whispering to the stars when pleading with the universe after kicking that guy to the curb. I knew that I would never allow another bully into my life again. What I didn't know was, how to actually avoid the same type of man.

So, I avoided men altogether and turned my focus inward. That's doing the work. That's deliberately taking the time to discover who you are and what you want while nurturing your sense of self-worth.

The thought of meeting someone else terrified me. I knew about the law of attraction, and I had worked hard at raising my vibration and strengthening my intuitive senses. Still, what if I attracted the same kind of man? What then?

Months and months later, I bought a pink pillar candle. I took a notepad and penned a list of all the qualities I thought was important in a lifelong partner at that time. It wasn't overly complicated. It wasn't unrealistic.

- Kindness

- Empathetic
- Compassionate
- Patient
- Tolerant
- Open-minded
- Respectful

Things like that.

A friend's Italian mother had given me some kind native "love prayer" that was to be performed on a particular date and time. I was to call on Archangel Michelangelo – the angel of love, and burn the candle over my list until it burned out entirely.

The morning arrived like any other morning. I did my normal thing and dropped my children to school. After which, I would come home to await the ritual hour. So, I began cleaning the house to fill in the time.

When I got to one of the kid's rooms, I saw him – Archangel Michelangelo. He stood still and beautiful in all of his 3inch glory on my son's dresser, and I had never seen him in my home before that moment.

The moments stalled and everything faded after that. I picked him up and held him to my heart and I couldn't help but cry as disbelief and utter amazement rippled through me.

Strange how things like that happen.

Of course, little Michelangelo took part in the love ritual I was to perform that day. He had a front row seat, and watched as I lit the candle and said the words out loud. The atmosphere was surreal; the room filled with an unearthly and loving energy that remained for the longest time thereafter.

When the candle burned out, I was to wrap the melted wax along with my list in a white cloth and keep it somewhere safe. I stuffed it under my pillow and that's where it stayed until a few months later when my husband entered my life.

He was everything I had wanted.

I'm not sure if it was the love ritual, or the inner-work I had done – perhaps it was a combination of both of these things. Intention and focus are a powerful affliction to adopt when we wish to evoke change.

Whatever it was, it was enough to raise my vibration and frequency to attract a partner who would always treat me respectfully.

As it turned out, my son had brought Archangel Michelangelo home the day before after visiting his father. That little guy became mine after that; he knows secrets only we two know.

23

5 SIGNS THAT YOU'VE HIT THE EMOTIONAL CHEMISTRY JACKPOT

Have you drawn the winning numbers?

The most vital component to kickstart a relationship would have to be emotional chemistry. Often described as a romantic spark, emotional chemistry is essentially the ambiguous and intangible phenomena shared by two people who feel a mutual special connection:

- The magical "click".
- The unspoken and energetic bond.
- The exquisite body rush.
- The chemical process simulating love or sexual attraction.

We can't force emotional chemistry. It is a natural and

undeniable connection. We either have it with someone or we don't.

According to relationship expert Susan Winter, "the early signs of emotional compatibility is that instantaneous "click" that we feel when we meet someone new. We immediately sense a connection that indicates we share a mutual understanding."

It's that deep sense of belonging. Your inner-voice that sings with the recognition of one of your own.

Chemistry can manifest in different ways, or not at all. We can land in the "No chemistry" zone, where we find it difficult to create rapport with someone. Or, we may find ourselves in the "bad chemistry" district where the harmony is nil to zero.

Meh. It's a part of life. I am certain that I possess an uncanny ability to rub a handful of people the wrong way. You've got to bury that stuff and move on for your own sanity. Definitely not the makings of a magical "click".

Let's talk about the good stuff.

Wikipedia says:

"Some of the core components of chemistry are: non-judgment, similarity, mystery, attraction, mutual trust, and effortless communication. Chemistry can be described as the combination of love, lust, infatuation, and a desire to be involved intimately with someone."

Ah … this sounds like the remarkable and beautiful bonds of a profound soul connection.

Perhaps I'm overthinking it ... sounds pretty good, though.

When we meet someone, it may be hard to differentiate between sexual and emotional chemistry, as both of these brain-inducing chemicals may evoke similar psychological, physical and emotional symptoms.

Since most of us are aware of the value of time, we tend to want to avoid activities and people that may waste this precious resource where possible. This is particularly true when our 20's and 30's are in the rear-view mirror.

Naturally, we want to know right away if the chemistry we're feeling is just sexual or if there's something more to it – something meaningful.

Here are 5 tell-tale signs that you've hit the emotional chemistry jackpot:

1. **Magnetism**

Have you ever someone and instantly felt drawn to them without any apparent reason?

I'm going to assume that you have at some point.

It may not even be a conscious thought. It's more in the vibes – the unseen energy between you that compels you toward each other and creates a deep sense of inner-knowing.

Familiarity. Belonging. Intimacy. Home.

It feels like all of those things and more. As if a tiny

ember ignites in the pit of your being that cannot either be fully articulated or explained.

Nor can it ever be unknown to you.

This person will possess your thoughts as much as you can feel yourself dominating theirs. The pull is extreme and undeniable.

1. **Easy Conversation**

Personally, I struggle with small talk. I can find it awkward, run out of stuff to say pretty fast and often say the wrong things that may be taken out of context. Deep and interesting conversations, however, fuel my soul.

When I meet someone and the conversation flows naturally, it feels miraculous to me. It's also a sign of emotional chemistry.

Mental connection.

This is when speaking to someone on this level becomes delightful. The conversation is easy, maybe even refreshingly challenging. Statements are understood - Even when opinions vary, there exists a mutual respect and acceptance for the other.

Effortless communication = incredibly strong intellectual chemistry.

In short, you just get each other and speak the same language.

1. **Silence is bliss.**

This is a biggie for someone like me. I cherish silence and believe there is nothing more satisfying than to just "be" with your lover without feeling the need to fill in the moments with mindless banter.

"Stay with me. Let's just breathe."

Lyrics from *Breathe* by Pearl Jam

You know when you share a special connection with someone when you can easily be silent together and just *breathe*. In fact, every relationship expert will tell you that the biggest sign that you've found someone significant is the fact that you are comfortable spending time in silence with them.

No forced conversation. No need to speak. No awkward silences.

And yet, your lover's presence remains powerful by your side, bringing a sense of mutual peace and joy within. Your love can be felt in the energy between you.

This is true love and emotional connection at its finest.

1. **The truth is in the eyes**

Sneaky glances. Locked gazes. The exquisite zing that catches every nerve ending and deliciously winds its way through your body when he/she looks at you.

The eyes cannot lie. They are the mirror of your soul.

You can barely keep them off of each other. You don't want to.

Even when you are together with other people, your attention and gaze will naturally seek out the other. Your other chemical half is your primary focus.

Our thoughts, emotions and feelings can be confirmed by the look in our eyes. Learn to trust what you see reflecting back at you in your significant other; the eyes will not fail to betray the authenticity of the connection - which gives the experience a beautiful and special kind of flavor.

1. **Sweet annoyance please**

I LOVE this one.

Someone once asked: *"Why so serious?"*

He may have been joking, but this is no … erm … joke.

The intention isn't to offend or to make the other feel bad. But damn, picking on each other for no reason at all is reason to play. Like an interesting word game. You want to provoke each other – you want to discover uncharted territory and know where the other stands in particular situations or topics.

Think of it as intellectual-sex.

It's fun, subtly flirtatious and creates intimacy in a bickering kind of way; and it's a secret language only you two know.

Knowing someone who you share the deep bonds of emotional chemistry is a magnificent gift in this world. For all the disconnection and separateness evoked by our fast and modern lifestyles, finding a kindred soul is like finding yourself in a world made for two.

Whispering souls together in harmony.

Time is relative when in the company of such a person. And yet, time has never been more precious.

24

4 WAYS TO MAKE HER FEEL SEXY WHEN SHE'S NOT IN THE MOOD FOR INTIMACY

She needs to feel like a woman if you want quality love.

*D*on't balk. If you're one of those men who constantly reminisce about the days when your woman used to swing it for you like Miley Cyrus on a *Wrecking Ball* because she's not eager in the bedroom, I'm here to tell you that no amount of nostalgia will bring back those steamy sex sessions.

The days of romping around in bed all day are gone. Life happens and so do kids, work, mortgages and households.

One of my girlfriends has been with her man for some fifteen years. Three kids. Two careers. Most of the household responsibilities are on her.

He gets to leave for work in the early hours to return

to a clean home, washed children and a hot meal every day.

She gets to leave for work after arranging the kid's morning routines and dropping off to school, returning to a home that needs upkeeping, kids who need help with their homework, a meal that needs preparing and showers that need to partake if she wants to keep her kids clean.

She does.

He goes to bed at 8:30pm. He even has an alarm set on his phone to remind him of bedtime. One evening a week, it is sex-night.

After a year of couple counselling, they eventually made a written agreement which covered an array of the issues plaguing their relationship.

She wanted him to stop drinking, be more considerate, help out more around the house and with their children, as well as curb his passive-aggressive tendencies.

He wanted Miley Cyrus back.

Huge difference. This was his number one (and two … maybe three) issue to prioritize his list of what he deemed the most important aspects in their relationship.

Sex.

Nowadays, if she dares to renege on her part of the agreement (E.g. Tired), the shit hits the fan in the form of pouting lips, child-like griping and persistent critical jabs followed by bouts of speech that begin with the words: *"Remember when you used to …"*

Two things:

1. A written agreement to sleep with your wife?
2. Memories won't bring back the passion, sir.

Neither will said agreement.

I mean, come on – it's not neuroscience. If you feel as if sex is lacking in your relationship, the last thing that is going to work to recreate the sensual flames is to uphold a written agreement.

How about some thoughtfulness? A little action … effort?

How about adopting a mature and growth mindset, and taking the time to learn what makes her feel sexy?

That's something a written agreement cannot produce. No matter how many times you sign the damn thing.

Each woman is different. What makes me feel sexy might not work for every woman, but isn't learning what makes her hot a tantalizing challenge to undertake?

We all want some pleasure in our lives. *A little sexual release*. Its natural.

We change. None of us are the same people we were when we first met, which means adapting and evolving is essential to a long-lasting and fulfilling relationship. Naturally this spills over into the love-making scene.

What made her horny years ago has probably revolutionized with her human development. Yours too.

I can't promise a *Wrecking Ball* scene, but let's

discuss some the hot stuff that may help to reignite her inner sex-goddess:

1. **Mind-F**k Her**

To the forward-thinking guy who seeks to give and receive pleasure from his woman, I couldn't think of a better way to begin than mental stimulation.

Women are wired differently to men when it comes to sex. We need to feel a certain connection. It ripples into the sex. Trust me.

You don't need a masters degree. You just have to bring something interesting to the pre-sex lingo.

Intriguing her mind will moisten her panties.

A need for mental connection is a must for many women in order to move ahead with her physical chemistry – this is true for new and for seasoned relationships.

When you get to the "loving" part, it's unbelievably mind-blowing.

It's like a sexuality continuum - desire begins and continues in the mind. When she is feeling connected and bonded to her man, the stimulation overflows into total love-flavored ecstasy.

1. **Use Your Lips**

I love lips. Even better when they're whispering in

my ear with your face close so that I can feel your warm breath and man-skin against my own.

It's just sexy.

It doesn't even matter what you say, so long as you say it.

Lips are especially good for kissing too.

Deep, passionate Frenchies. Light feathery body grazes. Sensual sucking.

Mmm.

Kissing releases the body's feel-good chemicals. I just discovered that thinking about it does too (mental stimulation right there).

Seriously, often the art of kissing is lost between long-term couples. Rekindle the passion with the gift of your beautiful lips. Make the moments count.

Lips are also particularly good for: Dirty talk. Compliments. Charm. Making her laugh – sexy stuff going on there.

1. **Erotic Massage**

Hello fingers.

Scented candles. Sexy vibes. Hot towels. Skin on skin.

You'll definitely want to make the oil an edible variety for where this scene is headed.

There is nothing quite like the sensation of touch to

kickstart arousal. Follow it with a helping of number 2 and it's more than happy days.

Benefits of sensual massage: Mental relaxation. Emotional rejuvenation. Sexual arousal. Stress relief. Helps to release negativity. Promotes intimacy and helps you let go of insecurities.

And besides, it just feels damned good.

Want to hear her moan?

Focus on her erogenous zones – the parts of her body with heightened sensitivity. This will create her sexual response.

Is it getting hot in here?

1. Be a Gentleman

Yes, being a gentleman is still relevant today and most women still like a bit of chivalry. We appreciate being treated like ladies.

From *10 Qualities of a Modern Gentleman* – Final Touch website.

"Today, being a gentleman is a matter of choice. It is a title you earn through an unwavering commitment to invest in your character. Gentlemen are not stiff, pretentious, or focused on elevating themselves. Instead, they strive to succeed while helping those around them succeed as well. Being a gentleman means that you care about how your choices impact others. It is about human connection."

I like it.

Being a gentleman encompasses many attributes. At its basic core, it is the desire to be graceful and respectful in your attitude and outlook on life.

This means throwing away things like written agreements, and accepting change while possessing a strong desire to be intimate with your woman because *you want to be with her* and not just because you want to get your rocks off.

The experience transcends into something much more meaningful when we really connect. Besides, fewer utterly mind-blowing sexual encounters surpass a quick fix anytime.

Make her feel like a woman.

She'll be putty in your hands.

25

I MARRIED A NARCISSIST. HERE'S WHAT IT TAUGHT ME

Charm. Friendliness. Kindness ... Narcissists.

*T*hey say you shouldn't associate with a narcissist. That you should avoid them at all costs. Anyone who does get involved with a narcissist is likely to sustain permanent emotional and sometimes physical harm. Yet, mental health website PsychAlive says "that the world is becoming increasingly narcissistic."

We may not realize a narcissist until it's too late.

That happened to me. I married a narcissist.

This was way before the whole "look at me" mentality kicked off with the social media networking of the modern era. Narcissists always existed. Even in the 90's.

But it's getting worse. Narcissism is now becoming a

widespread mental health issue. Hard statistics are pointing toward a narcissist epidemic in the contemporary world.

This doesn't make for good relationships.

Professor Brad Bushman of the Ohio State University: *"Narcissists are very bad relationship partners."*

I can certainly vouch for that.

The rise in narcissism means a potentially dire impact on our personal relationships. More narcissism means more narcissistic relationships.

Equaling more struggle and pain; more manipulative and game-playing behavior.

I didn't know that my first husband was a narcissist. I'm not sure that I'd ever fully made the connection between his behavior and Narcissistic Personality Disorder (NPD), until I was years invested in the relationship.

It might sound daft. Maybe a little naïve.

I wasn't accustomed to people who behaved in manipulative ways. None of my family members were inclined to exploit the feelings of others for their own personal gratification. None of them were self-absorbed, mean or egotistical. Everyone who was close to me were straight-shooters.

When they loved, they just loved. Simple. I love that about my family.

I think that when you are someone who doesn't know

or practice intentional manipulation, you tend to be blind when faced with someone who does. It's not in your database – you are unfamiliar with the language. So, you don't expect it from others.

When you encounter someone who is narcissistic, it hits you like an atomic bomb. *Boom*. Debris all around. You claw for your life and desperately scramble for shelter.

The charm. Friendliness. Kindness – The Narcissist.

This guy was finesse. He was very attractive – baby blues, perfect jawline … just the right amount of masculinity. Throw in a gentle demeanour and we have a killer combo.

He had style and took care of himself; his appearance and personal hygiene. A totally important trait in a partner if you ask me. No one wants someone whiffy.

He knew all the right moves. He knew how to make a woman swoon.

Flowers?

Check.

Dinner for two complete with candles and music?

Check.

Gifts made of gold?

Check.

Thoughtful, concerned and considerate?

Check. Check. Check.

Narcissistic people are passionate about the love-game. It's the nature of the beast. They show great interest in romantic prospects and proceed to enact out their seduction with generosity, expressions of love, flattery, sex and romance.

He had wanted me.

In hindsight, I realize that he wanted me for all the wrong reasons. He wasn't interested in me for the person I was on the inside. He had no desire to really connect.

I was a representation of his ego.

He said all the right things and I believed him. I gave him my heart.

"I love you more than life itself," he said.

But he never really knew what love was all about.

Alas, there were fleeting moments throughout the years when I would get a glimpse of something else beneath the fake façade.

Something authentic and ... humane.

I believed it was there. It's not that narcissists don't feel emotion. They just forget that everyone else does.

He hated to be vulnerable. Yet, it was in his most vulnerable moments that he felt real to me. Sadly, these were usually the same moments that followed a particularly traumatic ordeal. It was the only time he would appear sincerely apologetic for his behavior and how it impacted me. He might have cared on some level.

It never lasted long enough to make a difference, though. He would never follow through on his promises to change.

It can be difficult to know when you first meet and become involved with a person who qualifies with Narcissist Personality Disorder. These individuals are experts at concealing the qualities that may reveal their narcissist tendencies. I fell for it. Hook, line and sinker.

Let's flesh it out some more.

From Healthline: Narcissist Personality Disorder is a mental health condition characterized by:

- an inflated sense of importance
- a deep need for excessive attention and admiration
- lack of empathy for others
- often having troubled relationships

Furthermore, a person only needs to meet five of the following criteria to clinically qualify as a narcissist:

- grandiose sense of self-importance
- preoccupation with fantasies of unlimited success, power, brilliance, beauty, or ideal love
- belief they're special and unique and can only be understood by, or should associate with, other special or high-status people or institutions
- need for excessive admiration
- sense of entitlement

- interpersonally exploitative behavior
- lack of empathy
- envy of others or a belief that others are envious of them
- demonstration of arrogant and haughty behaviors or attitudes

I spent twelve years married to a hardcore qualified narcissist. Here's three of the most prevailing things the experience taught me about narcissism and myself:

1. **Say what? No Reasoning.**

You cannot reason with a narcissist. Very little makes sense in their world. When they were dishing up common-sense in-utero, I'm certain the narcissist wasn't around that day. At least, not my narcissist.

Effective communication was non-existent.

It's like your speaking to someone barricaded by an invisible screen constructed of ignorance and an acute incapacity to relate.

Impossible to penetrate but quick to ridicule and demean.

I learned how to hide myself - to conceal my vulnerabilities, my thoughts and musings, and to deny my true self to appease his vision of me.

My vulnerabilities were his power and ammunition. I learned how to protect them.

1. **Devalue - Twisted Tongues.**

A narcissist is a master at gaslighting. They possess the ability to inch into your mind and play with your sanity. Manipulative tendrils expertly seep into your thoughts so efficiently that you actually begin to question yourself.

Every word. Every action. Each gesture was his for taking.

Through emotional abuse and psychological manipulation, I learned to trust myself. I learned to be strong; I discovered the meaning of self-worth. Nobody has the right to devalue or use me as some kind of twisted amusement.

My thoughts *are* valid. My feelings count.

I learned to find and believe in my voice. I learned to value myself.

1. **Narcissistic Men are Really Weak.**

When a narcissist can no longer deal with a confronting situation; when they begin to feel out of control, often it is violence that becomes their next move.

Women and children are fair game. Men, however, are a different story.

I never told my family the truth about the abuse until I ended the marriage. He was wary of my brother; of other men. He knew if my brother discovered how he treated me that he was done for.

It's strange how we can protect an abusive partner. I know that fear is responsible for that.

Violence.

It breeds all kinds of negativity and disempowerment. But you have to be strong; you have to believe in a better life to get through. You have to know that it's not impossible.

I found my fire and learned how to stand up for myself. I realized that nobody was going to save me. No one could pull me out of that life except me.

Only I could protect my spirit and make change.

I dug deep to face my fears and find that extra strength; and I had to push past the threat of violence long enough to form a plan to get out.

I could make it happen.

And then, I did.

∼

Sharing your life with a narcissist is like existing in a warped world made of eggshells, guilt and self-condemnation. It's a shadowed life where everything is literally the opposite of happiness.

Connection is just something you read about.

Narcissists don't see the fault in their behavior and seldom do they learn from the past. It is as if people aren't real to them; that feelings are nothing but a narrative in a fictional story and you're their main character.

The woman who replaced me ended up in hospital. He beat her to a pulp.

If you asked him about it, he'd tell you it was nothing. He'd tell you that it was her fault; my fault; the fault of the girl who was before me.

Nowadays, I rarely think about those years. They belong with the wind. Yet, they are the same years that shaped the woman I am today.

A woman who sits down to write an article about lessons learned from a narcissist.

I hope they are wrong about the evolvement of a narcissistic world. I hope that more people will find a way to look within to discover their authentic beauty rather than to *"look at me"*.

Fool.

I would much rather look at someone who embodies the rich qualities of empathy and love any day.

Wouldn't you?

26

THE TRUTH ABOUT HONESTY

4 Things to Consider Before You Get Brutally Honest with Someone.

I'm not sure why people feel as if the truth needs to be delivered brutally in order to be effective. I believe that honesty embodies the qualities of love, matters of the heart and empathy, and that brutality and cruelty are elements that directly oppose the true meaning of authenticity.

Being honest is a virtue, but being brutal and cruel is not.

Honesty should never to be delivered harshly at all. It is a farce to believe otherwise. Furthermore, using honesty as a weapon to hurt others is unnecessary and uncalled for. You can be honest and kind without being hurtful and brutal with your words.

Time and time again, I have heard people say how they prefer to "tell it the way it is", but their beliefs and opinions about something are not the same thing as the ultimate truth.

Our perspectives vary. The way I see the world and filter my thoughts are not going to be the same way that you do. That doesn't make me delusional. Nor does it give you the right to negate or belittle me with your brutal version of the truth to appease your … erm … ego?

My husband is inclined to not sugar-coat the truth. Like, ever. He is blunter than a hollowed-out cigar filled with cannabis. This might sound counter-productive in the realm of self-liberation, but I often remind him that there is no need for him to *always* express his opinion about everything under the sun.

Naturally, his first reaction is to push back. It's in his nature. He's a classic Aries male who possesses a rapid-fire wit and rebellious personality; and he's a warrior for what he believes to be honest and true. He thinks about it, though.

He was able to understand that while honesty is important in a relationship, it doesn't have to be expressed harshly in order to make a point. He realized his abrasive manner was causing more harm than good in his relationships – with me and our children.

His hard messages were being buried under an avalanche of hurt feelings. Words can be so damaging. Words can kill.

As assertive and straightforward as he can be, I have had to learn how to match his strong personality traits with some fire of my own. Each time he chose to speak nothing but the "brutal truth", I'd show him another, more thoughtful way to express himself without the severity.

I can't be certain if it was my influence, but over the years my husband has learned to deploy a little finesse in his brash ways. He has learned that his truths do not always need to be voiced so forcibly, and that there is great value in thinking before taking the leap into brutal-honesty kingdom.

He cares enough to consider the impact of the way he delivers his words.

Brutal honesty can actually impede communication with loved ones rather than achieving harmony. It is also about telling the truth in a way that your partner will hear it and benefit from it. In this case, honesty needs to be tender. You can be present with your issues with some degree of gentleness.

Fact: Feeling strongly about your opinions doesn't make it a *fact*.

Being incredibly honest is not about being brutally truthful. I would even suggest that it is in your intention to be "brutally honest" that is actually holding back some honesty. You telling it like it is, isn't the same as how it actually is; this a fundamental misbelief and where we so often go wrong.

You don't have to compromise your honesty. There are ways to be honest and kind at the same time. We can honor the true meaning of honesty and deliver our truths with heart instead of brutality.

Consider the following points:

1. **Brutal honesty just tends to tear the person down.**

I know you've heard the phrase; *What Goes Around, Comes Around.*

Hell, Justin Timberlake sang a whole song about it and he is "Da Man".

There's no way around it - Your treatment of others will reflect back on you. Eventually.

So, before you feel the urge to be brutality honest, it is wise to choose your words carefully and acknowledge the other persons feelings.

It takes deliberate practice to actually separate facts from fiction. Focusing on facts — what we see, hear and observe — and then having the ability to avoid a kneejerk reaction long enough to consider the feelings of others, is what it means to be mindful – to practice empathy and invest in your character.

Keep in mind that brutal honesty isn't true honesty because the truth should never be cruel.

1. **Pause and Breathe.**

We've all heard the old saying: *"If you don't have anything nice to say, don't say it at all."*

There be truth in those words too.

Once you've said the thing, it's out there; forever floating around in word-land. Whether verbally, text or email - once they're out, you cannot retrieve those damaging words.

There are many different ways to say the same thing, and each version has a slightly different connotation to it.

Why choose to shred someone's soul when you can be just as effective by honoring and respecting it?

Sharing your facts and viewpoints with empathy and compassion means delivering your honesty without harsh dismissal, blame or confusion – victimless truth without brutality.

1. **Avoid the shutdown.**

We all know that person who believes they have the right to rip someone apart in the name of honesty.

It's a bogus mindset.

Delivering honesty in this way is when you shut yourself down from others and proceed to steamroll over someone else's feelings without acknowledging their emotions.

Being starkly aware that you may express your truths while simultaneously validating what the other person is feeling will go a long way in maintaining your empathy without compromising your integrity.

It will also soften the blow which will foster more positive and effective communication – they'll be more likely to listen to you and hear what you are offering. They will be more likely to accept your point of view and respect you all the more for it.

Positivity all around.

1. Honesty is not what you think it is.

Being honest has nothing to do with being angry, hurtful or mean. Letting off steam and venting is not the same thing as truthfulness.

Those emotions have very little to do with honesty, but for some reason we equate them with each other.

Being more honest is about being clearer; more specific; sincere; and more authentic. It's about hearing the other person, taking the time to understand their perspective and realizing their feelings are precious and thus, should be treated with care regardless of the situation.

- Honesty is about communicating your truths through acts of kindness and compassion.
- It's about human connection and spirit.
- Honesty doesn't require you to raise your voice.

- Truths don't need harsh derogative comments, threats or brutality in order to increase your honesty.
- You don't need to be more effective at stating the observable facts of the situation and your honest perspective about those facts.
- You don't have to be mean to be honest.

Remember, you can still speak your truth and honor your integrity without being mean or cruel to the other person.

The truth is: there is no limit to how honest you can be; only a limit to how brutal you can be.

You get to choose every time.

HOW TO SPOT A MAN WITH DECENCY

Why women can't find them and what to look out for.

"*Why can't I find a good man?*"
I can't tell you how many times I have heard a woman complain about the lack of "decent" men in today's world. Some men may have said the same about women.

This observation was made by women who have endured years of getting gipped in some form or fashion by the men they've allowed into their lives. Not even just for the long-haul variety. Fly-by's who play on the emotional strings of genuine people who desire commitment.

It appears connection and relationships between men and women have taken a turn into murky waters in recent times. As if the real meaning of love is lost on most of us.

So, what going on?

Honestly, while I understand where these women are coming from, lack of decency does not only favor men. Far from it. We exist in an accessible, consumer-driven and feasible world where nothing is unattainable in terms of availability and convenience. Even when it comes to our relationships.

Just about everything and anyone is gettable or usable these days.

We can even Tweet to the President. Where is Elvis when you need him?

"Out with the old and in with the new"

- A colloquial English phrase from God knows how long ago.

But surge forth into the future we must! Like all things innovative and cutting-edge, something must give in order to break new ground. Unfortunately, global reachability, online fluffs and puffs, and thrifty convenience has come at a high price on the human-traits scale — it has compromised some of our most vital qualities that constitutes a decent human being.

We've sold our soul to the highest bidder on eBay.

Electronics, cars, fashion … toilet paper anyone?

Is it a no wonder that our relationships are suffering in the real world when authentic connection is commonly replaced by a disposable mindset?

Blackballing. Ghosting. The "Big Chill" that demands we keep cool and pretend like we're not in it. The Pump and Dump and Smash and Dash. The bed warmer you dis to your friends on social media.

Feelings are a passing moment of uncomfortableness when the next-in-line is in sight. It's as if love and relationships have become expendable.

The reason why many women believe that decency is lacking in men today is because not every man has the tenacity, desire or stamina to go the extra mile for love when love is considered a dime a dozen.

Sure, things might be all rosy when we're in the initial love-cloud stages of a relationship. But when she becomes someone real with a real past and real expectations, the option to flip and run is as easy as a swift text message.

"Sorry, baby. You're getting too deep and it's not what I'm looking for."

Question: Since when has it been okay to break-up with someone via a text message, anyway?

Answer: Since the world became a digital copy of the real.

A fact that breeds lower values and stifles integrity, as well as accepting negligent treatment — all of which contributes to feelings of inadequacy and low self-esteem.

Expectations have never been so low. Neither has the capacity or ambition to evolve through deliberate introspection. A quick glance at some of the comments made on my article, *4 Things Women in Their 40's Really Want in a Man* proves as much.

For those men who instantly became offended at the simple qualities I'd mentioned in that article, I can only assume ignorance on their part. Some of these men were unable to understand the difference between women wanting a balanced and authentic connection, and downright criticism.

It's all in the mindset and maturity level — the ability to set the ego aside long enough to realize that relationships are not a power-play at some online bidding-war.

If you want to discover the magic of real love, you have to be willing to surrender all the way. It's not about one foot in and one foot out. It's not about tit-for-tat either. Love can't survive without putting your heart in — and I don't mean the cushy emoji you just flicked on her screen.

Fortunately, some of the comments the article received also shone a positive light on open-minded men who possess the ability to conceive and desire mutually satisfying and respectful relationships with women. Men who not only know what it takes to experience authentic connection, but also realize the importance and rarity of real love.

Real love and the ability to connect deeply begins with bringing back decency and desire for commitment. It's about being honest from the start. If we want to connect — really connect, we have to be willing to cultivate and embody the qualities essential for mature love.

Love rituals are not about roses, chocolates and cute emojis. Love begins from within and soars from the heart; and it starts by being a decent person in your relationships.

Decency in a relationship is many things. At its core it is respect and practicing humane qualities. Decency is recognizing when real love comes calling and honoring the heart of the woman who loves you.

So, what makes a decent relationship?

Simple. Decent people. Mature men and women.

Here are some "decent" characteristics to think about:

Modesty and Humility

Not in the narrowminded way of women's dress derived from Christianese dialect. I'm talking about the low-key character traits of humility and humbleness. Modesty is the ability to think of others before yourself, rejecting self-importance and living from the heart space.

Maturity is usually combined with modesty and humility.

You won't find this trait in the smart alecks, the overbearing know-it-all's or the self-appointed saviors. You find it in the unassuming and quiet — the guy who realizes the value in silence and reflection; whose heart is deeper than his "reputation".

Humility is not a weakness. It's a strong characteristic worth building on and one of the most important aspects a good relationship should possess because it demonstrates appreciation.

Humbleness between two people shows respect.

Sincerity

Forget the shams and apple-polishing. We all want to know where we stand with the important people in our lives. Truthfully, being a good person is not hard — if you're not looking for anything more than a fling, be upfront about it. Don't lead her on and mess with her head when you know her feelings are genuine and she wants more from you.

Be honest about how you feel — whether that's attempting to force something that's no longer there or declaring your commitment to the one you adore and desire.

It's the only decent thing to do …

Tolerance

I have my peculiarities and you have yours. No one sees the world in quite the same way, so why expect that of our lovers?

It is our differences that make for interesting and engaging relationships.

Tolerance is acceptance and an important component to decency. It's realizing the imperfections in your mate and knowing she is utterly perfect regardless.

This is love-in-practice. *Forgiveness and charity*. If

you're unwilling to go there, then carry on — no one is perfect in this world; least of all, you.

Tolerance is remaining gracious, considerate and courteous even when the pressure is on — and it plays a vital foundation to any true connection.

Wisdom

Qualifying sincerity, humbleness and tolerance with wisdom is the key to making the right decisions at the right time. A decent person with wisdom knows the value in a woman's love and will strive to honor her heart while guiding the relationship toward a meaningful reality.

Wisdom is ...

- Understanding how the world works and how to make potential change without producing unintended consequences.
- It's curiosity and expanding your worldview.
- It's acting in ways that are likely to produce the best possible outcomes for everyone involved.
- It's having the foresight to know what you need to do to make a potential future a reality.
- It's knowing when to say I love you.

~

In the broadest interpretation, being decent in a relationship means the capacity to be compassionate and love wholeheartedly. It's choosing to be honest and sincere with your lover, and implies acceptance of the fact that we all have weaknesses and we all make mistakes.

Decency is rejecting equivocation, arrogance and double-talk to make the distinction about what you really want from your lover and then having the virtue to act accordingly.

Real love demands decency; as does the woman who has given her beautiful heart to you.

28

BAD BOY OR ALPHA MALE?

The difference is in the Alpha-Flirt.

*D*o nice guys really finish last when it comes to women? The idea that heterosexual women may say that they want nice characteristics in a guy when what they really want is a bad boy is one of the most widely believed dictums of dating.

The notion is so wide-spread that you can actually pick up self-help books that teaches men how-to pick-up women by insulting them. The practice is known as negging — a tactic used by predatory pick-up artists to undermine a woman's self-confidence leaving her vulnerable to his advances.

Negging are those backhanded comments often delivered with a compliment. It isn't just a slip of the tongue or a mistake. It is actually a form of emotional manipulation that can be so subtle that you may not initially see it for what it is.

Urban Dictionary defines negging as: "Low-grade insults meant to undermine the self-confidence of a woman so that she might be more vulnerable to your advances. This is something no decent guy would do."

Umm ... you think?

Tapping into a female's insecurity and shaking her confidence as a means of "flirting" is extremely misogynistic, controlling and manipulative. Not to mention downright warped. But it's nothing new.

I used to know a guy who excelled at negging way before it was a thing. He was one of those guys who smelled like arrogance. You know the ones — attractive and self-assured to the point that he probably worshiped his reflection in the mirror each morning. He'd swagger around as if every female ought to be falling at his feet.

"You're way too nice for me ... you're way frigid ... I usually go for skinny blonds, but you're kinda pretty."

He was negging me. We ran with the same group of friends and he enjoyed teasing me about being a "good girl". He would either ignore me completely, or throw some kind of underhanded comment my way that made feel self-conscious. I assumed he just didn't like me, but every now and then I'd catch him staring.

It was utterly confusing. I actually thought that I wasn't good enough for him. I didn't realize it at the time but that's what he wanted me to think so that when he'd show me a soft moment, I would feel a surge of gratefulness and relief — *Maybe he likes me after all?*

～

Negging doesn't work.

Negging doesn't work. It's not arousing for women and its bullshit. Nobody wants to be around someone who makes them feel inadequate or gets off on power-tripping mind games.

Nasty innuendo be damned. Alpha males don't need to use such tactics to secure the heart of a woman.

Honestly, it's not that women are attracted to bad boys. We don't get off on getting involved with assholes. We do want nice guys, but it comes down to charisma, confidence, and social and emotional intelligence.

Sometimes, women may confuse an alpha male with a bad boy because bad boys ooze a certain type of seductive suave we may find appealing.

Flip it around to a man who comes across as ultra awkward, shy and timid, he'll stand little chance with a woman next to a man who has grace, confidence and poise.

Why?

It has nothing to do with wanting a "bad boy" and everything to do with instincts. All women are instinctively attracted to men with alpha male characteristics.

It has been an instinctual part of human nature since the days of our early ancestors, and it is nature's way of ensuring the survival of the species. Women seek to breed with men who are going to be good survivors and men seek to breed with women who are healthy and youthful looking.

Ultimately, a woman seeks to find a man who has what it takes to make her feel like a woman.

Characteristics like charisma and confidence are attractive in a man. These traits naturally flow into interesting, funny and flirtatious conversation.

Women love to engage with a man who *knows* how to talk to her. She wants real conversations that reflect her intelligence and demonstrate that you acknowledge her as a woman and as a person. The art of flirting is essential to not only striking interest and attraction in a woman but to also keep the spark alive in any relationship.

Most men talk to women in a way that only makes the woman feel friendly or neutral emotions. However, if you want more from your lady of interest, you have to make her feel sexually aroused by you. It starts by arousing her with your words and sincere flirting — alpha male style.

~

The Art of Flirting for the Alpha Male

Flirting can be an exciting and a terrifying experience. There is a certain vulnerability to sincere flirting as you are really putting yourself out there and expressing your interest in another person.

There is a complexity to flirting, too. We all have our own ways of expressing our interest in someone — what might seem like acceptable flirting to you, may come across as too aggressive and forward to your "loveliness".

It's like a complicated maze we have to work through.

Truth: A woman needs to feel mentally aroused before she can become physically aroused. Flirting shows her that you are interested and attracted to her. And like men, women respond favorably to positive and uplifting energy and not negging-tive energy.

The art of flirting with a woman works best when you …

Connect with your eyes — The truth is in the eyes and a woman who is interested in man wants to feel his focus and know she has his undivided attention. Sincerity is really conveyed by the way we look at each other when we interact. Making her feel important will open the doors of true connection.

Keep it playful — flirting is supposed to be light and fun, even when there is a sexual overtone to it. Keeping it fun allows her to relax and also gives you an opportunity to show off your sense of humor — and let's face it, all women love a man with a great sense of humor.

Make her smile — compliments are never wasted on

anyone, let alone the woman who holds your interest. I'm not just talking about her appearance — she probably already knows you find her attractive if you're flirting with her. A woman also needs to know you like her for who she is on the inside. When she feels safe in the knowledge that you like who she is, she learns to trust you.

Touch her — don't get creepy touchy-feely, but don't be afraid to reach out and touch her either. Touch bridges the gap between you and your woman, and gives her permission to touch you too. Just be mindful to keep your touch to her safe areas of her body: hands, arms and upper back are great spots to begin without making things awkward.

Be clear: Avoid the "friend-zone" — Men naturally want things to move forward while women may naturally erect the barriers when things are moving too fast. It is all about respecting and paying attention to her boundaries, but also making your intentions clear — that you want to be sexual with her. A woman needs to be aware of your interest or she will end up "friend-zoning" you.

~

Flirting is a fun. It's stimulating and wonderful part of our relationships, and an essential element in communicating our feelings and intentions to those we adore.

A woman doesn't need to be "negged" to be

successfully wooed and conquered. She won't respond to a man who wants to bring her down, at least not for very long. A woman just needs a man who takes the time to get to know who she is; she needs a man who sees, feels and hears her.

A woman just wants to love her alpha male without the BS.

29

4 NAUGHTY FANTASIES A WOMAN MAY SECRETLY WANT IN THE BEDROOM

Behind every good woman is a secret minx with a kinky fantasy.

*I*t is much easier for a man to ask for, or even just take what he wants in bed. When a man wants to switch sex positions, he just flips his lover over. If he wants a blowjob, he will subtly guide her in the right direction until he gets one. Maybe a threesome is on his wish list. He'll not-so-subtly suggest it after a few drinks one night. Even if she balks at the idea, at least he has expressed his wants and desires.

When it comes to sex, that's just how most men are wired.

While women's desire for sex is closely linked to the mind and emotional connection, for men, sex and desire begins in the body. They have massive amounts of testosterone coursing through their bodies; pushing and driving them toward sexual expression. Even so, most guys probably have one or two things they feel a little bit shy to bring up.

Maybe he gets turned on by something he watches in porn but will never mention, or perhaps he feels guilty or ashamed for liking something he wishes he didn't find as hot as he does. We all have our secrets. But, regardless of a man's shy or repentant feelings, I can assure you that it is just a small taste of what it's like to be a woman.

For many people, talking about sex in an open and honest way is not something they have much experience with. The thought may conjure all kinds of squeamish feelings and let's face it, no one wants to be judged by their significant other. We don't want to express a sexual kink only to be told that it's weird or "out of line".

During my early relationships, I seldom expressed what I wanted in the bedroom. It wasn't that I didn't have my own desires as much as I couldn't find the voice or the nerve to openly say what I wanted.

When I did find the courage to speak up, it was usually some half-baked version of the truth. This occurred for two reasons:

A. I was extremely aware of constantly keeping my partners ego in check. Which meant I was more focused on his pleasure and ensuring he didn't feel inadequate in any way. So, I would keep quiet when I wasn't as into something as much as he, or I'd fake an orgasm so that he would feel accomplished in his sexuality.

B. I was not confident enough to assert myself as a sexual being.

This is largely because society teaches and encourages men to be the sexual beings, whereas women are often shamed for having the same feelings and behavior. The classic double standards in action. We're all aware of how it works.

High school years showed me that the girls who slept around were "sluts' and the boys who played the field were "studs".

Society expects men to be sexually assertive and promiscuous. In many cultures, sexual prowess for men is even seen as a "rite of passage" into manhood.

Eddie Murphy famously embarked on one such journey in *Coming to America* when he left Africa under the pretense of "soaring his royal oats."

Over the years, I've grown into my inner "sex goddess". I have learned how to express my needs, desires and kinks without feeling dirty or ashamed. But the reality is that for many women, there is still a stigma attached around sexual expression and kinky confessions — concerns about rejection and ridicule from a partner is very real.

So, what changed it for me?

A journey into self-exploration and empowerment.

I slowly learned to accept my mistakes and flaws, and began being kinder to myself. I worked at letting go of what others and myself presumed was "right" and "wrong" about sex, and I realized that life is a collection of unrepeatable moments that were wasted on warped misconceptions.

Sex is a natural process of the human body. Desire is a part of who we are and a crucial element in our relationships.

Relationship researchers believe that the key ingredient in the sex-happiness relationship is positive affect, or being on an emotional high. Psychology Today concluded that "sex seems not only beneficial because of its physiological or hedonic effects ... but because it promotes a stronger and more positive connection with our partner."

So, we know that sex has an integral impact on our close relationships. We love, nurture and connect in the most deliciously intimate way through sex, and yet, we so often corrupt the notion of lovemaking through humiliation and judgment.

I decided that life was too short to wait for someone to give me permission to honor and connect with my own sexual power.

That didn't mean I went home with every man who hit on me. Quite the opposite. What it did mean was that I arrived at a place where I accepted and merged with my feminine energy in a very powerful way.

Getting Naughty Between the Sheets

Women can be a great mystery to men — particularly when it comes to sex. This is because we are told that sex isn't something we should want, and if we do, we must be sluts. We are told to be sexy, but not sexual. Great in bed, but not trampy.

From the onset we are drowned in a tsunami of mixed messages which makes being open about our sexuality difficult and complex. Additionally, women are often socialized to put other people's well-being ahead of their own — this gendered aspect greatly impacts the way we express and explore our desires.

This means that a man could be in a relationship for years without ever realizing his partner's fantasies. Eventually, many of her desires will be repressed and forgotten if she is not given the opportunity to give them a try. You never know what unexpected pleasures you both may end up enjoying together.

Partners need to feel safe to truly explore their desires, and communicating openly demonstrates commitment and intention.

If a man really wants to learn what his woman wants to try in the bedroom or what her sexual fantasies are all about, she needs to feel safe enough to tell him. She has to trust that he won't laugh, betray her or freak out, or even use her secrets against her later on.

Every woman needs a safe and solid place with her partner if she is to fully realize her fantasies. It's about building on the connection and layering the foundations of trust, communication and togetherness. It's be willing to share your own kinky desires and listen to each other.

What do you want?

Every woman wants to hear that question in bed. Actually sitting down and talking to your lover about what gets her hot and what doesn't can be a transformative and eye-opening experience.

Making the time to sit down and discuss bedroom antics is important because it encourages openness, assurance and acceptance — and those are vital characteristics to keeping your sex life healthy and exciting.

Each woman is different; as is the glorious rainbow of her kinks.

The potential for erotic fun is personal and differs vastly between women (and men), but there some fantasies that are common among women. With big love, a little finesse and a side of coaxing, you may discover something utterly intriguing about your woman.

Here are four common kinky fantasies that she may secretly like to try:

Domination and Submission

Some women want to submit to their partner, others want to dominate.

Alex Mantley from Ask Men:

"… but the truth is that at least some amount of a Dominant/submissive dynamic exists in most relationships, sexual or otherwise. Understanding how that works can bring both people in a relationship a lot of pleasure."

Dominant/submissive variations include:

- Permission to orgasm.
- Allowing your partner to orgasm.
- Deciding how they'll achieve orgasm — sex toy, oral, manual stimulation.
- Choosing the position, pace, location.
- Letting your partner control the moment.

Domination and submission can bring an exciting element of arousal to the relationship, but it's super important to keep the communication and consent flowing throughout the process. A submissive should always feel free to express displeasure and concerns.

Erotic Spanking

You may be surprised at the number of women who are secretly into being spanked during sex. If performed correctly, this kind of erotic spanking can take your sex life to the next level.

Reasons why women love to be spanked:

- Do we always need a reason?
- A mild (and hot) form of role play
- Amazing sensations

- The taboo element is a turn on
- She likes the idea of being "taken"
- She may consider the concept associated with passion and strong desire

Just make sure to set the rules and a "safe" word before you get started

Role Play

Roleplay is a fun way to explore sexual fantasies and desires. It's like putting on a costume for Halloween — it's fun to try something new and adopt a different persona for a while.

However, not all role-playing is about costumes. Sometimes just talking to each other through the scene can be very erotic. And statistically, couples who talk dirty to each other are more likely to enjoy better sex together.

Remember to arouse your partner's mind not just their body!

Temperature Play

She might like to spice it up with Fire and Ice. It might sound a little alarming but it is actually super easy and brings a nice kink to foreplay by introducing new sensations.

What's temperature play?

It's a technique often used in BDSM as well as ramping up "vanilla" foreplay using heat or cold to stimulate the skin and provoke a sensual reaction.

Temperature play is often combined with blindfolding and/or bondage to increase the sensation.

Temperature play is especially fun when hot and cold are combined together in unpredictable patterns, and can be a simple way to ramp up arousal. Just make sure to always test the temperature on another area of your skin before proceeding to the sensitive parts!

∼

And finally …

All women are unique sexual creatures who possess exquisitely naughty secrets waiting to be unlocked by the man she loves. No woman is more special than your woman — allowing her to express and embrace her inner sex-goddess will blow your mind … among other things.

Just proceed with love and tenderness, and have a whole lot of kinky fun!

30

THE HEALING GIFTS OF DEEP SEXUAL UNION

When we think of a powerfully embodied human, certain characteristics immediately come to mind. To be powerfully embodied is to have a deep understanding of who you are and how your actions affect others. It's the ability to manage your emotions and act from your authentic heart-center; it's being able to overcome your fears enough to follow your dreams and live your deepest truths.

Powerfully embodied humans possess attributes like self-awareness, integrity, kindness and empathy; they do not walk through life hurting others.

A powerfully embodied human is in touch with their sexual power and emotional intimacy.

An individual who possesses the above-mentioned qualities is also someone who is deeply actualized and expressed in their sexuality. In reality, it is uncommon to encounter such a person. Perhaps this is because taboo, narrow-mindedness and warped sexual hang-ups have managed to drench the purity and power of human sexuality and connectedness.

The true meaning of sexual empowerment has been lost on most of us beneath a tsunami of misconceptions, suppression and misuse.

None so much as the ultimate gift to man; the healing qualities of the sexually realized feminine — *Woman.*

We are keen get to the page to share our viewpoints about our experiences; lessons learned and the key take-aways. We're offering ways on how to live a better life; maintain healthier relationships; balance our mental health and make positive change. The key to unlocking personal empowerment and well-being can be discovered in a matter of clicks. Yet, rarely do we acknowledge the one and most important element to actually achieving true inner-connectedness — to each other, and to spirit and prosperity — the art of sacred sexuality.

"Sexuality is a superpower. The healing of sexuality is perhaps the most revolutionary step in the present healing work after thousands of years of suppression and neglect."

Dieter Duhm

Sexuality has a spiritual reality which plays a huge part in conscious connection, awakening and self-awareness. The link between sexuality and spirituality is strong and acts as a sacred bridge between our physicality and our soul. It is through sex that we discover and connect to the whole of the universe.

Through the ages, mystics have known and taught that sexuality is the outer physical manifestation of a spiritual urge to have mystical union with the eternal spirit. Tantric Yoga teaches that our natural desire and urge for sexual expression can become a means to union with source energy or God and is "at its highest level of human expression".

It is crazy-mad how much intellect and energy we use to suppress, hide and redirect our sexual energy. Equally interesting is that sexuality has been deduced to just a strong biological urge or the simple purpose to procreate. Time has tarnished the authentic sexual union to a gratifying, often voyeuristic or casual encounter. We have actually learned to feel shame about our natural desires, passion and longing.

The result has found us existing in an age where our desire for sexual connection has been downgraded to lower forms of sexual expression.

But none of this can diminish the spiritual significance or the real spiritual truth underlying the relationship between sexuality and spirituality. No amount of unawareness can actually omit the fact that sexuality itself is a sacred life force and the conceiving power in the universe — no matter how far suppressing female sexuality was the main tool of domination during the patriarchal era.

Carl Jung believed there was more to the libido than what psychologists had attributed solely to the sexual drive when he declared: "In truth, the libido is a life force or urge to life itself."

In its simplest terms, life force energy is the intelligent powerful energy from God or source energy to creation. It connects us to everything in existence and without it, there is no existence. Many cultures from ancient civilizations up until modern day science have been aware of an energy surrounding living organisms.

We know that this higher-intelligent energy exists.

~

The Healing Gifts of the Sacred Feminine.

"Woman has so much to bring to this planet once she is loved upon and supported. She is here as a powerful service to love and life. But we have spent history mishandling her. Raping and pillaging her resources, controlling her; assuming that she is limited. She is not limited. Woman is entirely unlimited when she is of aliveness. Powerful sex is a method of stoking the fires of life within. It keeps us alight."

Chris Bale — Master Energy Worker, Sexual Alchemist and Spiritual Guide.

A woman who is well-sexed is like the most lustrous star in a night sky. She is a creative force who thrives and glows to her natural rhythm; she is alive and obvious, and she carries a certain type of magic that unfurls, transforms and embellishes everything she touches.

A well-sexed woman soars above all, but she is almost elusive.

Bale, who has had many years of experience assisting countless women with energetic initiation says: "There are cornerstones of a man's development; sexual understanding and implementation is a huge part of the greater whole. Really learning how to be with a **woman's body and soul is a true art form** which requires deep listening and a commitment to presence.

Learning to be and to stay present with her is where our healing exists … do not underestimate the necessity of figuring this out. It will grant you a very different experience in this life."

Chris Bale is a man who has come to realize the sacred power and healing in the feminine. A rarity among men who understands that a woman who is deeply in touch with her feminine sexual power is a like blazing flume — a love-channel of life, spirit and pure healing energy that allows, in full freedom and trust, to energetically express our joy in life and find healing in the sacred union.

Being loved upon is like soul syrup to the feminine. Deep sex with a conscious and present man is like medicine.

Consider the following script from Tamera — *Sexuality as Sacred Power:*

LOVE IS THE ROAD TO EVERYWHERE

"Before patriarchal religions introduced the concept of sex as "sinful," which they used to dominate people, ancient tribes saw Eros as a natural path to connecting with the sacred. Ancient feminine mystery knowledge placed women at the center of the tribe, where they could connect to nature and the goddess and practice fertility and sexuality rituals. To people living in harmony with the natural rhythms of the Earth's cycles and all life around them, sex was part of the sacred practice of transformation."

Deep sex is embodied with deep nourishment.

A transformative healing takes place when a woman is well-sexed by her "present" man. This is because deep penetration and intense connectedness supports and guides a woman back to her core. It creates contemporary pathways toward the heart and body. It unleashes her from stress and anxiety and keeps her connected with her vibrating orgasmic consciousness and spirit — all of which she needs to remain in health.

Bale goes on to state that: "You are dealing with a beautifully wild and insatiable love monster, who's staple is conscious-cock with heart."

This is done through a man's capacity for presence; through deliberate and present sexual union.

Essentially, we are talking about two people coming together in absolute fusion to make high forms of love and intentionally tap into the healing power available in the spirit of true sexuality; lovers creating the space that allows us to trust, connect and touch upon the euphoric pleasures and essence of the universal reality of sexuality.

There lies the path and power of true healing for humanity; and there exists in all its wonderful glory the key to true self-realization and empowerment.

I cannot help but agree with Bale when he mentions *that* "every woman wants to feel her man's reverence and honor between her thighs — She wants her heart to be f**ked wide open via his love; his conscious-cock and his firm connection with heart."

"She wants to feel your Godliness, and she longs to drip down upon it, feeding your deepest essence with her nectar."

Imagine a world when we begin to actually figure it out?

Start figuring it out. Please.

HOW TO TELL IF AN INTROVERTED WOMAN IS INTERESTED IN YOU

Here are 6 sure-fire signs to look out for.

It took me a long time to figure out and accept that I was an introvert. For some reason, I had figured being an introvert meant that I lacked important attributes that made for an appealing human who could easily relate to others.

Attractive personality qualities like energetic social skills, assertiveness and vivaciousness. I was never the "life of the party" type, preferring to keep a low profile and observe.

During my younger years, I found it difficult to strike up conversations with my peers and form friendships. I was quiet and reserved, choosing my people wisely and treasuring them all the more for it. When it came to guys, for a very long time I chose no one at all.

That didn't mean I didn't have crushes — I did, only nobody else knew about it. I discovered early on that guys liked me. Perhaps it was my quiet disposition and my unassuming nature, or maybe they just found me attractive. Whatever the reason, it has taken me a lot of years; inner-work and building on experience to be able to feel comfortable around the men I find attractive, and then actually express my interest in them.

An introvert woman is naturally hard to crack. She tends to build invisible walls around herself that only a few select people are ever permitted entry. Like all introverts, she excels at observing. So, when she is interested in a man, she will meticulously find out more about him — she'll quietly study his moves, habits and personality; assess his ways; interests, nuances, dreams and lifestyle before making a choice as to whether he might fit into her world.

Chances are that an introvert woman may come across hot and cold at first. This is usually because she may struggle with finding her social "middle ground" of communication with you — she won't want to freak you out by spending too much time with you, but she won't want to shut you out either.

If, at times, she comes across as aloof, snobby or indifferent, its usually more about a case of the nerves and/or clamming up, and less about being uninterested.

Personally, I have always struggled with overcoming my naturally shy tendencies. So, when I realize that I'm falling for a man, my first instinct totally goes against all "mating" protocol — I clam up and avoid him like the plague for a while.

Why?

Because my logical brain knows that feelings of attraction merely skim the surface in a potential mate. For the introverted woman, there must exist deeper and more meaningful qualities in a guy for her to move forward in the relationship. She must be able to trust herself with him, and trust that he will honor and respect her feelings.

If she's anything like me, she'll need the space and time to process what she's feeling and more importantly *why* she's feeling it.

Once she's established how she feels about you, she will be ready to test the waters some more — tediously perhaps, but ready nonetheless. Her moves and signs will be subtle and at times may leave you utterly baffled about what's really going on. Keep in mind that her deep and star-gazing world is unique and quirky; and worth every bit of the effort it takes to become a part of it.

For those men who have an introvert woman in their life but are a clueless as to whether or not she is interested in you, here are some signs to look out for:

She stares

But it will most likely be horribly awkward because the only thing she's got on her side when you're around is her ability to "think" — direct eye contact may distract her from her usually fast working brain. She will take every opportunity to study you in-action when you're not in direct conversation with her.

Introverts crave to know things — she's usually always in research mode, so you'll most likely catch her glancing or frowning over at you quite frequently.

Questions are her love language

When an introvert woman doesn't care about someone, she couldn't care less about their favorite songs or greatest fears. If she genuinely likes you, she'll want to gather as much information about you as she can — this means she will dive deep and go for the big stuff — dreams, desires, philosophy; what your MBTI and star sign is (so she study up on those and learn how to communicate with you).

She'll also be interested in the insignificant's; throwing you random questions that may surprise you — and she *will* remember all the details.

She will shut up and listen.

Introverts love talking to people who seem interested but if you are talking about something and she just listens intently and even encourages you to keep talking by asking questions, that means she is very interested in what you have to say and wants you to know that.

Honestly, even though an introvert woman has probably already thought up any idea you procure — she will willingly listen to your ideas and love every one of them.

At the other end of the spectrum …

She may try and debate you intellectually. If an opinion or argument is stated, many introverted personality types will love to play devil's advocate to gage just how much you know on that subject. But don't be offended if this happens because this may be her way of acknowledging your intellect and actually complimenting it — she wouldn't try so hard to prove an idiot wrong.

Sometimes she may actually agree with you, but just likes to see you in your philosophical, intellectual state. Sigh.

She shares her deepest thoughts and dreams.

Typically, introverts don't usually talk about personal topics with just anyone, preferring to discuss more general things. This is because she needs time to emerge from her shell and reveal her true self. If she begins to talk with you about her feelings, interests, ideas, likes, and dislikes, this means she's into you and feels comfortable being around you.

It also shows that she trusts you to understand her. Introverts are very used to being pushed under the rug or misunderstood, so if she has the guts to finally open up, even about insignificant things, she likes you. Big time.

She shows you that she cares.

Introverts are loyal when it comes to the people they love and cherish. She will be attentive to you and show you a great deal of care and compassion if she considers you to be a part of her inner-circle.

She will love to spend time on her own — this is her way of keeping her inner-world balanced while processing her thoughts and emotions. So, if you're invited into what appears to be her personal space to spend time with her there, this is a definite sign that she enjoys your company and is interested in you.

~

Despite her need for deep introspection and dedicated world-reflection time, your introvert woman is a creature just like you — she really does like to spend time with the people who matter to her and she's not as hard to read as you might think. You just need to pay extra attention.

DOES A WOMAN'S BREAST SIZE REALLY MATTER?

A woman's relationship with her breasts is complicated.

emale breasts have been a source of fascination for eons. And for good reason; they are a sensual and enchanting part of the female form symbolizing life-giving and creative force qualities such as birth, nourishment and fertility. In our culture, breasts are also commonly associated with the femme fatale; seduction and femininity; comforting promises and sexual fulfillment — Women's breasts are among men's favorite sex toys.

Ancient cultures may have practiced Goddess worship and regarded the female form as the source of all life, but the "source of all life", wonder and pleasure is not always what it's cracked up to be — women the world over experience all kinds of personal issues with their breasts.

The relationship between a woman and her breasts is rarely neutral, and it begins at the onset. As a teenager with brand-new budding breasts, it wasn't long before I took to wearing oversized sweaters in an attempt to conceal and ignore them. I still considered myself a kid and frankly, I was comfortable staying that way. I didn't ask for my chest to suddenly explode; I wasn't woman. Yet.

What did these swollen mounds of flesh want with me, anyhow?

The thought of wearing a bra caused a volcano of mixed feelings — On one hand, I knew that I was on the threshold of the new and exciting world of womanhood, on the other, I wasn't so sure that I was ready to grow up.

It also meant that I had to accept the inevitable — the not-so-thoughtful taunts of my younger brother who occasionally found twisted pleasure in yanking the back of my bra strap when he was frustrated with me. *Humph* — baby brothers can be a pain in the butt at times … but so can big sisters.

The truth is that women are just as obsessed with boobs as men. Psychology Today reports that only 30 percent of women feel satisfied with their breasts, observing that: "Younger and thinner women worried that their breasts were too small, while older and heavier women were concerned about droopiness."

That's 70 percent of women dissatisfied with their breasts. Thank goodness for the push-up bra and America's number one cosmetic procedure: breast surgery.

Ah, the breast-surgery Gods of America; here to fix, stitch, mend, and reposition nipples ...

It's totally valid, especially when considering the media-driven imagery we are forced to swallow — *what woman doesn't aspire toward the vision of a sun-kissed beach-babe-lifeguard whose inflated breasts bounce like perfection as she runs along a shoreline in search of ... erm ... a life and death rescue mission?*

Hmm...

In her time, the famous blond sex symbol with the critically-acclaimed rack was no-doubt in part responsible for an upsurge in breast implants, as well as igniting inadequacy in small-breasted women the world over.

Which begs the questions — do straight men really prefer bigger breasted women? Does boob size actually factor into our relationships?

Researchers have never actually explained why men devote so much head-space to breast fixation, speculating that "humans evolved the fatty deposits around the female mammary glands for sexual reasons."

Anthropologist Owen Lovejoy argued that evolution put a bull's-eye around both female and male reproductive organs in order to promote pair bonding, and Live Science says: "Another long-standing

KIM PETERSEN

theory holds that breasts evolved as a way to signal to men that the woman attached to them was nutritionally advantaged and youthful — and thus, a promising mate."

After I accepted the life sentence of bra-wearing and got comfortable with those strappy pieces of underwear, my budding breasts began pushing their way out of my chest like no tomorrow. Seriously, those girls just kept growing and growing … and growing. Until they became the source of much male ogling.

More uncomfortableness.

I can't tell you how many times a man has had a conversation with my breasts when addressing me. No, they don't talk back and my face is further north, thankyouverymuch.

It's a bit like Homer Simpson drooling over doughnuts. I'm not bragging. Quite the opposite. My breasts and I have had a life-long turbulent relationship — one which has seen me curse them and then finally grown to accept and love them.

But it's not just me, women complain about men looking at their breasts when talking to them all the time. And just ask any waitress; she will tell you that wearing low-cut tops with a visible cleavage means better tips. Then there's the age-old joke about a group of women with various degrees of qualifications applying for the same job. Who gets hired?

The woman with the largest breasts.

They may look nice, but having large breasts isn't all

218

perks and wildflowers. The fact is, big breasted women do have a complicated relationship with their boobs, too. I can certainly vouch for that.

For one, do you realize how difficult it is to find a sexy piece of lingerie that comes in a larger cup size?

Extraordinarily hard. It's like searching for a real-life leprechaun.

Ditto for feminine-looking bras. The pretty lacy ones are seldom made in Double D's and upward. Nope. We commonly face a depressing and limited selection of bland granny-style bras, so we are forced to shop speciality if we want something sexy.

Don't get me started on strapless bras ... they're a no-go. Full stop.

Clothes shopping can be an ordeal too — dresses fit wonderfully until you get to your breasts and they become a mashed-up version of flesh and nipples. Not. Attractive.

Button-up tops are challenging. So are swimsuits.

Running is not our friend ... no, really ... we are *not* Pamela Anderson doppelgangers.

So, yeah — all women have their own personal relationship and battles with their breasts — and it isn't just limited to those women who have smaller boobs and wish for more than a handful.

Large breasts equal eternal trials, challenges and inner-conflict, too: "My face is up here, dude." ... "No, I

won't show you my breasts in exchange for a drink —
what the?"

True story. Jerk.

Okay, so we know men like breasts. It's a no-brainer.
But do they actually find bigger boobs more alluring?

During our early days together, I'd frequently catch
my husband sporting a goofy grin while wearing my bra
on his head. He had been utterly stoked that the cup could
fit snugly over his skull. Go figure.

I am not a man; he is. I recently asked him the
burning question. His dark eyes swept over my breasts
and he smiled:

"Large breasts are lovely — yes. But so are all breasts
— period. At the end of the day, it's not the size of a
woman's breasts that men find alluring as much as
the woman attached to them."

And there it is … small, large or in-between, breast
size isn't all that important when it comes down to it —
not when love is involved. Unlike breasts, love cannot be
faked.

Moreover, a woman's breasts are intimately
connected with the forces of the heart connection: linking
her to love, compassion and wisdom — whatever shape
or form.

What man in his right mind could deny such a
precious, life-giving gift — especially when attached to
the woman he really loves.

33

DEAR MEN: YOUR BEARD MAY BECOME ITS OWN LOVE-DESTINY

*L*et's clear this up once and for all — beards are sexy. And frankly, it is a damn shame to a see a man who is capable of growing a nice spread of facial hair forgo his God-given stubbly gifts to the razor.

But there *is* a catch — I'm not just talking about any kind of beards. Certainly not the unruly, extra-long variety that conjure disturbing thoughts of what might be breeding among the wiry tangle. No.

Lord, no.

The kind of beard I'm hitting on is the simple but effective full-trimmed beard or the gorgeously heavy stubble. Either will do just fine. In fact, a write-up at her.com states "that a neatly trimmed full beard tops the list of things a man can grow on his face by virtue of the fact that it shows he has the patience to grow a beard and the wherewithal to keep it neat and tidy."

Appealing. Sexy. Attractive.

Beards are much more than just a fashion statement or the ever-contentious subject in the domain of male grooming practices. From Grizzly Adams to scruffy day-old stubble, they are essentially a manifestation of a man's masculinity and imbued with social messages.

I have been asking around; getting the facial-hair low-down with some of my lady friends. Turns out, I'm not the only woman who cheers and celebrates the heavily stubbled jawlines of our male counterparts. There are others; many others. Women everywhere find beards incredibly tempting and as it happens, studies report that beards can play a significant role in a man's love life.

Researchers from the University of Queensland in Australia gathered data from 8,520 women and concluded that: "Overall, the women said the sexiest men were those sporting heavy stubble, followed by short stubble. Men with full beards and clean-shaven men were rated the lowest on the overall sexiness scale."

Hmm ... sexiness scale. I like it.

The heavy stubble or well-trimmed beard has been said to make a man appear confident and approachable, too.

A quick pause and worth reiterating: Do not confuse the alluring, well-trimmed beard with the scruffy snack holder where you store crumbs and other food morsels that it happens to catch. You know, the full-blown beards that might tempt you to decorate with seasonal ornaments come Christmas time.

Please don't do that.

And please consider removing the porn-stache if that's your thing, too. Think John Holmes and then think again. The early pornographic actor's life may have been measured in inches but in this case, the inches work against you.

I mentioned as much to a brief love-interest of mine when I had first started seeing him some years ago. I know, it sounds a bit … erm … mean, but he was really out of touch with the what-goes of facial hairdom, and he wasn't nearly over 50.

Brief pause: Dear men, if you're over 50 you have earned the right to do whatever you like with your facial hair, with the exception of a soul patch (the small tuff of hair between the lower lip and chin) and the goat patch (extended version of the soul patch).

Anyway, love-interest quickly took to the razor and emerged from the bathroom with an upper-lip that resembled a freshly plucked chicken. Porn-stache was gone but something was terribly off … the clean-shaven look just didn't suit him. Nor did he feel comfortable minus the lip rug. So, he embarked on growing and maintaining a nice heavy stubble.

And it was sexy.

It's not just women who prefer bearded alpha males — men also prefer men with facial hair. The same study revealed that "men feel more masculine by growing a beard — had higher levels of serum testosterone, which was linked to a higher level of social dominance. They also tended to subscribe to more old-school beliefs about gender roles in their relationships with women as compared to men with clean-shaven faces."

Another pause to contemplate a few cool bearded men: Hello, John Lennon. ZZ Top. Gandalf. Jason Momoa. Brad Pitt and … Santa.

The authors of the study theorize that for women who are looking for a long-term mate, beardedness may be more attractive as it "indicates a male's ability to compete for resources."

Many women tend to associate more masculine faces with physical strength and social assertiveness, finding men with facial hair to be attractive and dominant, both socially and physically. The beard enhances these traits in men and is a strong representation of masculine energy.

Kind of like the Yin and Yang dynamic between the sexes.

Most people know or have at least heard of Yin and Yang. Yang is masculine and Yin feminine. Everything contains Yin and Yang energies, including each of us. They are two opposite yet complimentary energies.

The ancient Taoists believed that every relationship is a complex balancing act, namely balancing Yin and Yang.

Furthermore, Yin is what makes you want to receive sexual energy from another person and Yang is what makes you want to initiate sex with your partner. This suggests the underlying primal need for women to be naturally drawn toward bearded men; to balance her femininity, if you will.

And there may lie a man's love-destiny and self-fulfilling prophecy — in the lovely folds of a well-groomed beard.

Having said that, I am starkly aware that some men have difficulties growing facial hair, or just plain prefer the clean-shaven look. As does some women. All of which is totally fine. So long as there are fewer neckbeards and Fu Manchu in the world, we're all winning.

34

HOW A MASKED-LOVER LOVES YOU

Love behind a mask is never going to get real.

I like to believe that there is good in every person. When I say that, I'm not just talking about the surface kind of stuff that makes for pleasant exchanges and niceties. Anyone can do that. It's a behavior we learn at the onset if we want to "fit" into society and successfully interact with others.

Most people want to be seen as a good person.

One of the most challenging and difficult lessons that I have had to learn during my life and continue to be confronted with is the fact that not everyone knows how to be a good person.

Not deep down. They may exhibit good qualities, yet, these are pushed so far behind their "mask" that anything truly authentic they may express is often fleeting and construed with lies.

The other thing that significantly correlates with this lesson is this: just because you may be a good person doesn't mean that everyone else is.

That's where we so often trip up — because good-hearted people tend to view the world differently to those with hidden or deceitful agendas. Good people don't think in sneaky or conniving ways; they don't seek to gaslight, exploit, abuse or devalue other people. A decent human being doesn't set out to trick and manipulate the emotions of another. Therefore, those shady thought processes and behaviors are not in a "good" person's natural repertoire — they don't expect to encounter that which doesn't align with them.

Does that make sense?

I'm not saying that I am perfect — not by any means. None of us is perfect and that is the beauty of experiencing life through the lens of humanity. We get to screw up; we are supposed to fall and fail; say the wrong things and make regretful decisions. We are to here to bleed and then heal; and to feel the raw reality of the earthbound creatures we are.

All of these experiences layer the fabric of our personal growth and yet, if we can't transmute these lessons, failures and heartache into something meaningful and learn how to relate and connect to each other with heart and authenticity, then we're not really grasping the bigger picture. We are choosing a masked existence over gritty, glorious and real-life experiences — over real love.

Love behind a Mask.

I once fell in love with a masked man. What I mean is that he had erected much of himself behind walls. His comfort zone existed in the confines of his inner-world, and he was accustomed with only sharing surface pleas-antries with most people.

I'm an introvert, so I get that. But I also understand that we must reach for more and step outside our comfort zones if we are to truly experience the love and connection the world has to offer us.

It was the kind of love that creeps up on you; the kind you feel stirring deep in your soul when you first meet but cannot quite grasp the intricate depths until it begins to unfurl through your being with an undeniable truth.

I was able to see him; really see him and his beauty beyond his mask — and he was the most wonderful and loveliest human being I'd ever had the pleasure of encountering.

Perfectly flawed.

My love was powerful enough to penetrate his layers and glimpse his soul. Real love has a way of doing that, but even a love like that isn't always strong enough to completely blow the mask.

Was he a good person?

I believed that he was good; I sensed his heart and felt his real self; I knew him in-soul, if that makes sense. Yet, what I saw as a beautiful gift caused him to react in ways that revealed the opposite of everything precious and real in this world — his fear of becoming vulnerable and embracing the love we shared saw him taking actions that translated as exploitative behavior.

It was love from behind a mask.

A masked-lover will do things like this:

He will use your heart as a game

Callous, calculating and downright mean — the masked-lover will play on your heart strings to elicit your emotions as some kind of ball-game; and the worse thing is, is that you fall for it because your love is real and knows no ugliness or thwarted concepts.

To the masked-lover, it feels as if your heart is nothing but a recreational past-time that makes for twisted amusement. He doesn't seem to care how he hurts you when the focus is on the rush — the ego-driven "fix" that appears to stoke his warped, unclear intentions.

Does he love me, or does he love me not?

Unfortunately, getting his "fix" lands on your sleeve.

He will use your love against you

Blatant lies, obvious confusion and off-beat comments designed to cause you to second-guess yourself — in a word; Gaslighting.

A masked-lover excels at using double-meaning phrases, planting seeds of uncertainty and lying by omission; withholding significant amounts of the truth and/or weaving snippets of truths through the words he knows you want to hear.

Is he real or is he not?

So skilled is he at achieving his objective, that you find yourself feeling hopeful that your loved-one is finally getting real — a glimmer of happiness drifts through you … you want to believe; *oh, how you want to believe!*

The moment you do is the same moment he will drop the sword and crush your heart. Again.

His terms — he sets the rules

Life behind the mask is seldom one of inner-peace. That is because he has had a taste of true love and he cannot forget you. He may even resent you for disrupting his life; for making him feel more than he ever had before you.

He knows how much you care and love him — he is drawn to those loving emotions as he senses the profoundness; the deep soul-truth and undeniable connection in his heart. Yet, he will only allow you in so far — and only in a way that is suitable to him and his agenda — challenge his boundaries; seek validation and transparency, and you risk the sting of his venomous bite.

Will he bite or will he bite me even harder?

It doesn't feel so good.

Naturally, when you are in love you want to know exactly where you stand — the masked-lover has no stable place for your feet, and he won't catch when you fall ... you're on own, baby.

He will polarize you

Using others comes easily to people who exist behind a mask. You may have something he or she desires — a skill-set or a gift, something they lack, want or require in their life — it could even be the way you see the world and/or the way you open your heart to love. Whatever it is, they'll want it until they don't.

You'll happily go with the flow, offering all that he wants because your heart knows no limits when it comes to the man you love. Hell, you'll even feel grateful that he wants you as a part of his world in some way — despite that deep in your soul you know that you are more deserving than the crumbs he is dishing it out.

Will he break me, or will he protect me?

Then it happens — he finishes with you — he chews you up and spits you out faster than a stick of gum and you're left polarized from a world you were once part of.

He breaks me.

~

What can you do if you are in love with a masked-lover?

I used to believe that love was powerful enough to

overcome any obstacle. The truth is that love *is* the most powerful, connecting force within and around us. Yet, I've learned that love isn't always enough when it is treated negligently.

Sometimes, we may be forced to protect our heart from those we love the most.

To endure loving someone who clearly has difficulties accepting and expressing such deep emotion, may mean that you need to walk away and/or have firm boundaries for your own sanity.

Love isn't always easy but it should never be soul-destroying or rife with games. It should never be devalued or used, or come at the cost of your self-respect or dignity — no matter how hard you love someone.

If people aren't willing to change, then you cannot change them and neither can your love.

Some people will go through their entire lives hiding behind the masks they have created for themselves, choosing to run and hide when true love comes calling in favor of playing it safe. Yet, something deep within compels them forward, if only to experience love through the tainted version created from the lens of a mask.

Masked-lovers may feel as if it is too risky to lay down their weapons and accept the gift of true love. When the reality is that true inner-growth and healing can only happen when we become vulnerable enough to embrace the journey; forfeiting such a beautiful and precious endowment will result in stagnation — and there is where the masked-lover feels safe … and perhaps faces a life of eternal loneliness.

If we really want to live a fulfilling and meaningful life, we have to be willing to ditch our masks and get real; we have to be willing to fly.

35

HOW TO SHOW AN INTROVERTED WOMAN THAT YOU CARE

Have you got a little spare time?

*S*ome introvert types struggle to express and explain their thoughts and emotions outwardly, particularly when it comes to their deepest feelings. This can become even more of a challenge when they are unexpectedly confronted by high-level emotional situations and relationship issues. Well, that's me, anyhow.

They say that men usually cringe when their woman utters the words, *"we need to talk"*. I am no man, but when my husband says those words, my first reaction is to run for the hills. I hate that phrase.

In my marriage, the tables are turned in that department: it is he that sometimes complains of my lack of emotional availability and those pesky avoidance issues.

Give me a bucket of sand and my head will dive right in.

Yes, I can be a clammer-upperer. Thankfully, my husband has learned much patience when it comes to me. He knows that he needs to give me fair warning if he wants to address anything heavy because he is aware that openly expressing and receiving emotions is not always my strongest suit. This is just how I'm wired (INTP here), and while he sits at the other end of the communication spectrum, he respects that.

The thought of sitting down to discuss how we're both "feeling" conjures all kinds of uncomfortableness. It's not that I don't want to express myself out loud, it's more that I sometimes have trouble explaining my feelings — especially if it's on the fly and unexpected. I need process time.

Give me a laptop and a blank screen, and there is my comfort zone. I'll fill in the blanks while carefully sifting through and analyzing my feelings because that way, I have more control over the output and time enough to articulate my emotions without the ... erm ... emotional part getting in the way (who am I kidding? I'm a writer).

Writers, huh?

That being said, you might want to thank your lucky stars that not all introverted women are like me in the emotional-expression department. I am certain most introverted women may be more comfortable talking emotions. And while I can appreciate that sharing those delicate expressions is an important element in a relationship and worth fostering, I am much more comfortable showing someone how I feel about them.

Actually, showing is really where its at, isn't it?

We can say as many words as we like but they mean nothing if we don't back them up with our actions. Showing is in our nature; our physicality and the heart we bring. It is true that the way we treat others is a reflection of our inner-worlds. At the core of any healthy relationship is respect, consideration, compromise and compassion.

So, when my husband feels as if we need to talk about something, I will make the time to listen to him even if it makes me feel uncomfortable because I know its important to him. The fact that he will first give me the space to collect and process my thoughts, shows me that he cares enough to allow me that freedom to be who I am without pushing me into a situation that feels awkward to me.

My first husband had a completely different approach to my introverted nature and idiosyncrasies, often becoming frustrated with the way I expressed myself. Which only caused me to withdraw further into my shell and eventually shut him out altogether.

Unlike my current husband, he was unable to comprehend our differences; or rather, the way that I see and interact with the world. So, he took to belittling me and making me feel ashamed that my communication could sometimes become awkward. He would mock me because I found large social gatherings challenging and draining.

Obviously, this was a man who didn't understand the beauty created through our diverse personalities. Or that our unique perspectives and differences allows opportunity for growth. Dissonance and challenge are wonderful tools for expansion.

The other thing was that he never actually saw me; basically, holding his own idea of who he thought I ought to be — an idealized version of someone who *wasn't* me.

Introverted or not, a man has to know his woman if he is to make a strong connection with her. If he knows who she is then he will understand how to show her that he cares. Here's how to show your gorgeous introverted woman that you care a bucket-load:

She Needs Quiet-Time

This is a must-have. It's no secret that introverts need ample time alone. Most of us need the space to get our "hermit" on and your introverted woman needs time alone to recharge her batteries. After which, she will be ready to join back in and get her social on again, with you.

Just because she cherishes her alone-time, that doesn't mean she loves you any less. In fact, she will love you all the more for respecting her much-needed respite from the world.

Authenticity is a Must

It is so rare to encounter someone who isn't afraid to tell you how they feel. Although some introverted women may have difficulties in the way she expresses her own feelings, truthfulness and honesty are very important to her and she needs to *know* that you care about her. Don't be afraid to open up.

She has enough going on in her head without trying to figure out where she stands with the man in her life.

And ditch the games. No sound adult appreciates them. Just saying.

Patience Will Get You Everywhere

Patience makes all the difference in building vital relationship components like trust, acceptance and communication.

She needs someone who has the capacity and desire to be patient in learning who she is and how she expresses herself. If she's anything like me, she could be affectionate and wild one second, then completely disappear for the next several thousands.

This behavior might seem erratic at times, throw you off guard and completely baffle your mind. Think of it as an intriguing part of her introversion and put in some patience — remember that much of her life is spent absorbed within the confines of her inner-world, so don't be afraid to reach out to her and let her know you're still around. She'll appreciate that more than you probably realize...

Intimacy & Connection

Introverts are born to connect more deeply than others.

Despite my own struggles with feelings, doesn't make them any less present. In fact, introverts are deep thinkers, therefore we feel deeply and care deeply, its just that sometimes we may become overwhelmed with the intensity of our feelings — which impacts *how* we express them.

It's very rare that an introverted woman will trust someone enough to let them in. So, once she feels close to her lover, she will appreciate the moments in which she experiences a rush of emotion and boundless connection to him.

Deep down she is a highly-sensitive human being who longs to connect with a kindred spirit; and she recognizes the value of stepping out of her comfort zone in order to experience true love and connection.

Be there for her and you will reap the rewards of introvert-style bonding.

Quality time

This kind of circles back to the beginning. *Time.* It is what you both need to fuse your energy, nurture your connection and become real *lovers.* The part where get to be your unique blend of each other.

Above all else, this is what she wants and needs — to know all of you and in every way possible.

When an introverted woman is in love with you, it is *you* that fills her thoughts and dances across her mind's eye. You who is her muse, her dreams, future and fears; and the fascinatingly endless puzzle she loves to explore.

But doesn't everyone who ever truly loved?

Honestly, these points aren't really just about what an introverted woman needs to feel valued and cared for. They are elements we all need to thrive as individual human beings and offer the best of ourselves to the world and the special people in our lives.

Then, we give each other the most important and precious gift of all — our time.

Beautiful, wonderful time.

ABOUT THE AUTHOR

Kim Petersen is a USA Today Bestselling author of the new *Blood Legends* series, *The Ascended Angels Chronicles*, and co-author of the Stone the Crows series. Her debut novel, *Millie's Angel* received a gold award in the 2017 Dan Poynter's Global eBook Awards.

Kim's nonfiction work has taken her down an unforgettable journey through co-authoring *Creative Writing Energy*, to a fun stint with podcasting, to becoming a top writer on Medium in Love and Relationships. Currently, she is working hard with a special friend at creating a unique online publication called *Living Out Loud*.

Connect with Kim directly by subscribing to receive her emails, so that you don't miss out on the exciting launch of a very cool publication about real life now.

Click here to subscribe and collect your free copy of Life. Death. Love & Connection while you're there: https://forms.aweber.com/form/33/1858665233.htm

KIM ON SOCIAL MEDIA

Medium:
https://medium.com/@kpetersenwrites11
Website: http://bit.ly/kimpetersen
Facebook: http://bit.ly/2MdNLjK
Twitter: https://twitter.com/kimpetersen_
Amazon: https://amzn.to/2APcSF0
Bookbub: http://bit.ly/2Tt8weC
Goodreads: http://bit.ly/2EJ7K58

If you enjoyed this book, please consider leaving a review where you purchased your copy – thank you!
Kim.

Click here to subscribe to hear more from me and collect your free copy of *Life. Death. Love & Connection* while you're there: https://forms.aweber. com/form/33/1858665233.htm

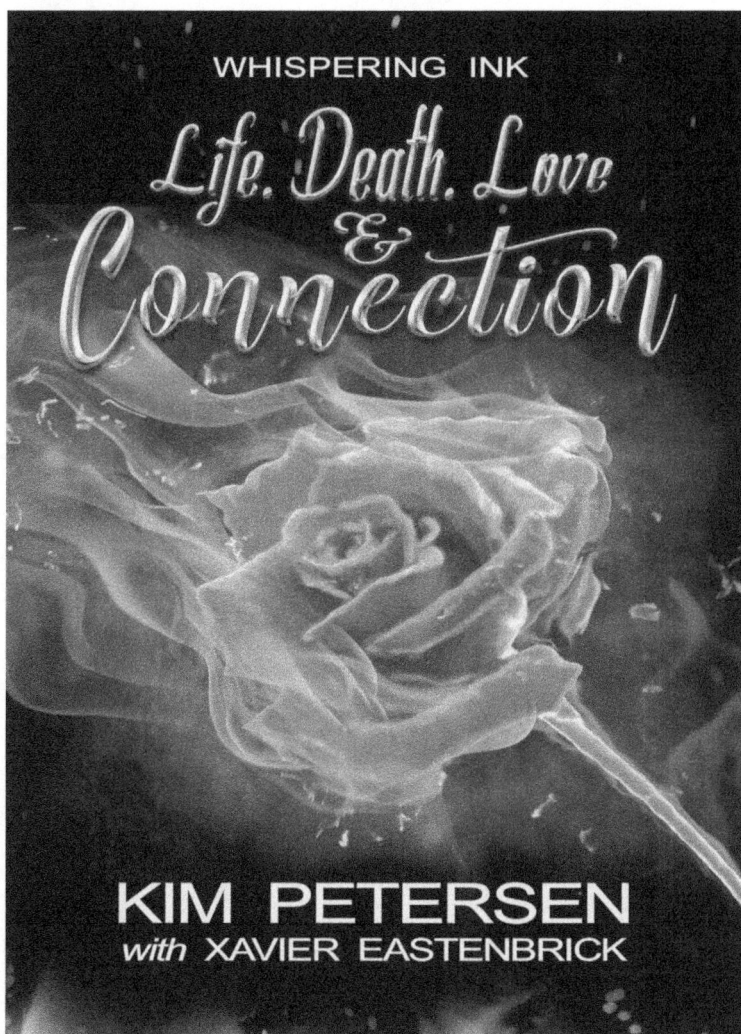

WHISPERING INK

Life. Death. Love & Connection

KIM PETERSEN
with XAVIER EASTENBRICK